# Smart Girls
# Marry Money

⚬⚬⚬

ELIZABETH FORD

& DANIELA DRAKE, MD

RUNNING PRESS
PHILADELPHIA · LONDON

9   8   7   6   5   4   3   2   1
Digit on the right indicates the number of this printing

Library of Congress Control Number: 2009922153
ISBN 978-0-7624-3517-3

Cover and interior design by Jason Kayser
Photo research by Susan Oyama
Edited by Jennifer Kasius
Typography: Mercury and Verlag.

Running Press Book Publishers
2300 Chestnut Street
Philadelphia, PA 19103-4371

Visit us on the web!
www.runningpress.com

# TABLE OF CONTENTS

Please note that all of our stories are true,
but some characters are composites.
After all, we had to protect the identities of
the guilty and innocent alike.

Smart girls don't like to be sued.

CHAPTER 1

# First Things First

*Most women use more brains
picking a horse in the third at Belmont
than they do picking a husband.*

LAUREN BACALL, *HOW TO MARRY A MILLIONAIRE*

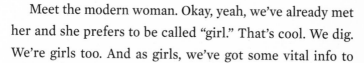

Meet the modern woman. Okay, yeah, we've already met her and she prefers to be called "girl." That's cool. We dig. We're girls too. And as girls, we've got some vital info to report.

After attending a few class reunions we noticed many lady lawyers, doctors and MBAs were still slaving after forty, while lots of less brainy gals were taking long vacations from their day jobs, shopping at Prada and enjoying more than their fair share of hot-stone massages.

We asked ourselves, "Why do (some) bimbos fare better than the smart chicks?"

Having taken a whirl or two in the love dance, we found ourselves wishing that someone had warned *us* of the pitfalls of falling in love, marrying the wrong guy or the agony of divorce. Why didn't Mom tell us? If your mother *did* bother to give you any solid advice on life, like most daughters, you probably weren't listening.

Since we think of ourselves as smart girls, we often like to support our ideas with research. And one of our favorite well-supported observations is this: *People are more likely to take advice from strangers than from their friends or family.*

So listen to us, because we care, we really do. Here's the bottom line—whether you're drop-dead gorgeous, skinny, fat, or even if you think you're just plain *fugly*♥—we girls have one big obligation to ourselves and our families:

### Find your fortune while you're young and marry a man with money.

Buttressed by experience, we use cold hard facts, real science and true stories that back up the case for what we call:

### The Gold-Digging Imperative—"The GDI"

---

♥ fug•ly [fuhg-lee] *Slang: Vulgar.* As defined by UrbanDictionary.com, "fugly" is a term used when someone is "*more* than just ugly."

We don't think "gold-digging" should be frowned upon. Why, we wonder, does society applaud a girl who falls for a guy's "big blue eyes," yet denounces one who chooses a man with a "big green bankroll"?

What's the difference? Earning power is, after all, a reflection of his values and character. Big blue eyes? Not so much.

The average guy believes most gals are only looking for money, but the truth is too few of us are interested in their income at all. The modern gal is earning her own cash and is looking for emotional security.

Too bad it doesn't exist.

What's worse, national statistics[1] show women suffer far more economically than men when marriages fail. With this in mind, we have some advice, and please take it in the gentlest possible way: Girl, get your head out of your ass. Instead of looking for love, let's look out for our own security, the kind you can count in dollars and cents.

Now we're not saying that money equals happiness. Everyone knows even the very wealthy can be downright, even bitterly, miserable. This is not about "happily ever after." It's about being smart and avoiding economic disaster by clinging to old paradigms about love and marriage.

Marrying for money isn't new. In fact, throughout history spousal arrangements have rarely taken any other form. In the past, marriage was primarily a system to promote the financial, social and political aspirations of the families involved. But these days society is pretty much disgusted at the thought of a mercenary marriage. A smart girl needs all the facts, and she'll have them when she finishes reading this book.

But money means nothing without our soul mate, right? Most smart girls long for it. From the day we're born we're immersed in a culture that elevates romantic love over . . . pretty much everything else. And with true love as our highest goal, marrying for any other reason has come to be seen as just plain wrong. Immoral even.

We're not all down on love. We know falling in love is yummy . . . all you need is love . . . love is patient, love is kind . . . love means never having to say you're sorry. Unfortunately, instead of strengthening the bonds of matrimony, social commentators predicted that marrying for love would drive the divorce rate right up around 50%.[2] And they turned out to be right.

When couples started to marry for love, soon afterwards they also sought the right to divorce. The reason? If *being in love* is a valid reason to marry, then *being out of love* is a valid reason to divorce. Turns out, romantic marriage and divorce are just about the only pair that's still together. If this trend continues, the term "lifelong partnership" may soon be retired— except when referring to certain animal species, like wolves.

To prove our case, we present a lot of data and statistics, but if that's not your thing, feel free to skip ahead to the naughty parts—there are plenty. You may ask, "Why so much sex in a book about marriage?" Because sex is the reason for our existence. It's *the* primitive biologic act, driven by our ever present animal instincts that color and influence almost everything we do. The more we thought about it, the more everything seemed to boil down to one thing: the F-word.

Or, as you'll see: F-words.

### BOTTOM LINE

Don't just be smart, act smart. Get to work!
Dust off those gold-digging tools and marry well.

**CHAPTER 2**

# Fiction: Having It All

*We live in fictitious times.*

MICHAEL MOORE, FILMMAKER

Before we plow into a full-blown discussion about love, let's first tackle the modern gal's mandate to *have it all*—a great partner, a brood of exceptional children, a well-run household and a high-paying/meaningful career . . . all at the same time. The problem with this seemingly excellent idea is that once we actually *do* have all these wonderful things, life can get rather overwhelming.

Over the last four or five decades, somehow the boys on Madison Avenue have convinced us to worship at the altar of *having it all*. However, many of us have found that *getting it all* often costs more than *having it all* is worth. Why? Well, partly because for working gals, *having it all* often means *doing it all*—and it's difficult to be a serious professional while wearing three-inch heels and a thong.

On the other hand, many men focus first and foremost on *having a great career*—and then maybe a hot wife (yes, she must be hot) who'll take care of all the rest. As a Harvard professor asserts in his book *Manliness*, "Men and their success at work are intertwined."[3] For many a man, the end of his career equals the end of his identity, and retirement becomes a hellish purgatory. We love men and want them *to be themselves*. If a man and his manliness are intertwined vis-à-vis work, then we are here to help.

Let's review:

- *Men are built to make money.*
- *Smart girls should exploit this.*

Before you get your panties in a bunch—don't get us wrong—we know women are more than capable of making a living. We believe in equal rights and equal opportunity and all the great things that the women's movement has given us. But we can't ignore the way things have turned out. We girls are all the lucky recipients of the hard work of the women who came before us. We believed their promises and pinned our hopes on the twin dreams of *having it all* and *happily ever after*.

But those dreams *didn't* come true for a lot of gals—hard-working post-feminist women who are feeling more than a bit fed up. Here's the story of our friend Georgia, a case in point.

## Super Freak

*Georgia earned a degree in business administration and eventually landed a job with a furniture manufacturer. Within a couple of years she was practically running the company, although above her were two tiers of male executives who seemed to do nothing at all. She was thrilled with her career, but deep down what she really wanted was to find her Prince Charming. When she met Aiden at a nightclub, love blossomed when each confessed their secret addiction to highly experimental sexual practices and the music of Rick James.*

*They wed but put off having kids because of Georgia's busy schedule. Aiden had dreams of being a successful landscape architect, but in reality he worked on and off as a gardener. Aiden looked good, shirtless and sweaty, while pruning the roses in front of the house. So although Georgia was tired, she didn't mind working out every day at the gym to stay sexy for her guy. She didn't even mind paying the bills.*

*Then, three years later, one of her do-nothing managers fired her on a technicality and replaced her with someone's do-nothing nephew. She had crashed into the glass ceiling she swore never existed. Months later, Aiden moved out. While she had been busy selling truckloads of computer desks and climbing the Stair Master to nowhere, he had fallen in love with a girl he met at the community gardens who, like him, was passionate about eradicating chemical pesticides. (As for her sexual practices, Georgia never found out.)*

*Suddenly, Georgia was jobless, exhausted, and totally alone.*

Georgia had drunk the Kool-Aid of our times—a combination of the sweet powder of romantic love plus a quart of happily-ever-after, with a jigger of workplace success, shaken until her brains were stirred. She awoke with a hangover and has yet to recover. Why? Because she believed that her competence and hard work would translate to workplace rewards, *and* she deeply revered the myth of Prince Charming.

Just like all of us, she thought *it* would never happen to her—but it happens all the time. In relationships and the workplace, tossing the old broad out is commonplace. Loyalty and honor are out of place in our disposable culture: Women are often easily pushed aside, replaced with more lithe and malleable versions of themselves.

You've probably heard some version of Georgia's story before. Has modern society stuck it to us both ways? Empowered young females work harder to look sexier than ever, while they carry far more than their fair share economically.[4] Meanwhile, men have been allowed to become slackers who deliver less and less. That's probably why more than a few of us are dreaming of early retirement and popping antidepressants like Skittles.

Nevertheless, we have good news. We've figured out a plan:

### *Use your sex appeal to score a man who earns while you're still young.*

It may sound harsh, and it is harsh, but it's true. Let's highlight the reasons:

- Your sexual power is unstoppable when you are young.
- You may not believe it now, but you will get older.
- You will get tired.

- You won't want to work so hard at your job, or to stay thin and beautiful.
- It's still a man's workplace and for the vast majority of women the glass ceiling is practically bulletproof.
- Even if you are successful in your career, most women need a second income to really make it to the Promised Land of financial security.

It's time to start treating your life like reality, not a fairy tale. We live in a world that runs on dollars and good sense. The GDI can prevent a future that no smart girl believes will happen to her. We're not saying become Anna Nicole and go after some old codger just for his wallet (unless that's what you're into). We're saying find a man to enjoy, to have fun with, be intimate with, and all that girly jazz. Just remember to take economics into account. It's a move toward financial security.

So even if your husband leaves you for someone younger or you get sick of hanging out with your old man, with a few bucks in your pocket you can live well, pursue a successful career, and still have a shot at "true love."

## BOTTOM LINE

Marry well while you're still young.
It's a smart girl's best chance to "have it all."

## CHAPTER 3

# FemiNasties

*That's the trouble . . . a sex symbol*
*just becomes a thing. . . .*

MARILYN MONROE

———— ∞ ————

Before we go any further, we need to stop and give a nod to the current culture:

## Live Nude Girls!

In our new extra-raunchy, pornographic society, we're not only privy to a dog's-eye view of some celebutante's stubbly snatch week after week, but we also watch co-eds pull down their panties in Snoop Dogg's cult video classic *Girls Gone Wild: Doggy Style*.

Don't get us wrong, we're down with the Dogg, but the new norm may be slightly shocking to many a smart girl. And it's not like you can avoid it—these days, you can't wait in line at a grocery store without being bombarded by sexual images of half-naked celebrity tarts. Author Ariel Levy, who coined the term *raunch culture*, calls these sexy girls *Female Chauvinist Pigs*, in her book of the same name. According to Levy, a female chauvinist pig is "post-feminist. She is funny. She *gets it*. She doesn't mind cartoonish stereotypes of female sexuality."

On the other hand, we think these young women are, in their own highly sexualized way, modern-day feminists. They do exactly what they want and they don't care who doesn't like it.

We call them FemiNasties.

How can a smart girl who's tuned into pop culture avoid it? Even the fairytale princesses are now more like Playboy-style mermaids wearing seashells on their tits. Mattel has a line of Barbie paraphernalia called, "My Scene Juicy Bling," described in the *Los Angeles Times* as "child trollop figurines."[5] Informed by these expectations of womanhood, many a smart girl cultivates her sexiness to highlight what she believes are her most powerful assets. But if she doesn't know better she may just end up as the objectified sex toy.

We don't mean to preach—okay, we do mean to preach—so listen up. To the chagrin of many parents, it's commonplace for pre-teen girls to dress like hookers to get attention from boys. (If you're a young teenager reading this, yes, we're sure you think you look absolutely awesome dressed in skank-wear.)

But no matter how ubiquitous dressing slutty may be today, male attitudes towards sluts haven't really changed that much in the new millennium. Back in the day, a fast girl was whispered about, her reputation ruined. Now she's likely to get something even more public and long lasting: not a guy's undying love, but an internet posting of her in a highly compromising position.

Thanks to the World Wide Web, Nastie-ness is more widespread than it used to be. But it's not a brand-new trend. Our old pal Serena was a FemiNastie before everyone else started to dress like ho's, too.

### Serena the Siren

*Serena was a classic hottie back when pubic hair was still in style. She was tall, with ivory skin and strawberry-blonde hair, which she dyed to match "down there." She trimmed her bush to create a perfectly symmetrical heart shape that drove guys wild.*

*Serena frequented upscale dance clubs on the Sunset Strip and turned heads as she table-hopped wearing her trademark emerald-green miniskirts that barely concealed her bottom. Her plunging necklines often revealed a nipple even before it became de rigueur. Serena was always seen with the movie stars and moguls. They took her to exotic countries on their yachts and private planes, where she drank only the finest champagne.*

*Serena enjoyed being sought after and fought over. She laughed at the notion of being tied down to only one of her many suitors. Glancing over her shoulder to watch the scores of men in hot pursuit was one of her favorite pastimes.*

Serena used her allure to get what she wanted at the time—close encounters with famous and powerful men. Her sexiness was her power. Noted sexologist Theresa Crenshaw describes the thrill of being desirable in her book the *Alchemy of Love and Lust*, "[A sexy woman] is so irresistible that *he* loses all reason . . . Control? She has it. He lost it. He is her conquest . . . This is a power-over-men fantasy."

So these days, the girls who "accidentally" forget to wear their undies are simply exploring one aspect of their power. Some may say that girls have gone wild, but it's actually the guys who go wild over us. In fact, the guys have gone so wild over us that the owner of the Girls Gone Wild (GGW) franchise became an overnight millionaire.

But here's the rub—it seems all of the owners of these types of explicit video franchises are men and they often get the girl-talent for free. Sometimes the girls receive a hat or

T-shirt. The men make off with the loot and go play golf on the French Riviera, while the stars of their shows are shacking up five to a room in seedy beachfront motels with semen stains on the carpet and bedspread.

So it's still true that the power equation doesn't add up. But with knowledge comes power, and we believe we may be able to flip that script. Many people interpret all this flesh flashing as a backslide from the rights we gals have gained over the last half century. But we disagree. We think it's just a rest stop, a bump in the road, a booty call, if you will, on the long road back to where we belong—being properly subsidized by our men while we take our clothes off.

Okay, so maybe all of us don't have to go that far. But all this sexiness is not a cultural crisis deserving of condescension, disappointment and endless hand-wringing. Like it or not, it's the playing field where we play out the modern game of life.

Overt sexuality—and in particular images of half-naked women dripping with sex,  drive our economy. Cleavage is power. Prostitution flourishes at the high and low end. Porn powers the Internet. Sex sells cars and beer and scads of girly magazines, tv shows, film and sports. Can you imagine pro football without those bouncy breasted  cheerleaders? We want sexual "equality" but let's face it—you don't see so many *men* out there shaking sex at women to get their attention—the *Sexiest Man Alive* issues may get a nod, but *Playgirl* is a joke to most of us.

Men lure us in other ways: trying to be manly and powerful by earning money and being successful . . . and did you notice they just *can't keep their eyes* off that woman who just walked by—an ex-playboy model in a short white dress.

So Nasties, go ahead and be nastie. But don't forget that even the sexiest girls grow old—that is, if they're lucky. So if you're into being a FemiNastie, remember your hotness is a commodity. Don't just spend it for the sake of being admired. Instead, try to use it to get something tangible you can take into your old age. After all, there's nothing more tragic than an aging Nastie standing in the unemployment line.

## Serena's End Game

*Our sexy siren Serena woke up at 46, tending bar at the same swanky club (now under new management) where she had once sashayed with attitude. She joked that she'd forgotten to raise a family. It occurred to her that none of those seemingly ardent prospects had ever proposed marriage. By then we were all getting bored with her stories of celebrity sex. Especially distasteful was the one about the aging theater legend giving her a golden shower (now that's just plain old nasty).*

So whether you're a Nastie or among those still keeping tops and underwear on, you need to be smart because you won't be the hottest girl in the room forever. All girls need to look ahead and fight for their financial futures. It's okay to use your FemiNastieness—but don't let it use you up.

## BOTTOM LINE

Raunch may rule the current culture,
but smart girls can still win.

## CHAPTER 4

# Falling in Love: Temporary Insanity

*People love . . . because they can't help it*

STEVEN PINKER, PH.D., *HOW THE MIND WORKS*

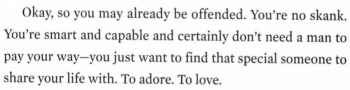

Okay, so you may already be offended. You're no skank. You're smart and capable and certainly don't need a man to pay your way—you just want to find that special someone to share your life with. To adore. To love.

We've all devoted a lot of time pursuing that crazy little thing called love. All gifted storytellers—poets, songwriters, novelists, movie makers—know the power of a great love story. Few among us can deny being obsessed with the fantasy of finding a soul mate, and the embers of romantic love keeping us warm forever.

Sadly, our research[6] has shown that wasting our youth and beauty pursuing romantic love is a bad bet—a search, you might say, for fool's gold. And yet, we want to believe in it, because it feels so damn good.

## Basic Instinct

How does that magic happen? What is "falling in love"? For centuries the philosophers, poets, scientists and pretty much anyone who's ever been dumped have sought the answer. Yet to date no one has come up with anything we can bank on—and that is, after all, what the GDI is all about.

Some psychologists believe love can be activated by reigniting pleasurable memories from infancy and child-hood.[7] This might explain why some guys prefer big butts to large breasts. Our friend Teddy claims he fell in love with his voluptuous girlfriend because her enormous boobs reminded him of the comfort he received as a child from his big-breasted grandmother. Another friend, Will, is attracted to boyish stick-figurines with no breasts at all. (He may be gay . . . but we digress.)

Once interest is piqued, all those feelings of attraction, desire and yearning thrum along until you find yourself feel-ing more than a little queasy—not sleeping, not eating, heart pounding, hands sweating, stuttering, and with an ache in your chest something akin to pain. You didn't choose it. It rose up within you and took over your waking thoughts. It hurts. Yet you can't help but savor this exquisite affliction— this mixture of pain and delight. Suddenly, you find you can no longer deny it: You are hopelessly in love.

You are helpless.

Many scientists now say romantic love is like a primal urge. Anthropologist Helen Fisher likens it to a drive strong enough to override almost all others, including the need to nourish yourself, rest or attend to your family, friends and sometimes even your children. The quest for romantic love is a basic instinct so powerful that many a smart girl will lose all rational thought and become victim to cons and slackers who only want to take advantage of her youthful search for "The One." Beautiful young Maddy had to learn the hard way.

## S.T.I.M.

*Madeline was a book smart girl who earned a good living in real estate in the Orlando area. She excelled at work, but her mom used to say that her "real job" was president of a company called S.T.I.M.— Sorry Taste in Men.*

*Maddy was a head-turner: heart-shaped face, thick blonde tresses, and a body they used to describe in the South as a brick shithouse. Anyone could see that she could have her pick of men, but she always found "chemistry" with losers. The worst time was when she "fell in love" with a lad called Christian. They met at a dinner party and he was charming, cute, and a successful financial manager to boot! They became inseparable.*

*When she told friends that she'd found "The One," they smelled a rat. His story didn't add up. Why did he need to borrow her car? Why was she paying for their romantic dinners? Worried for Maddy, her friends called the international brokerage house he claimed to work for. Naturally, the Human Resources department had never heard of him.*

*Even with all the evidence laid out before her, the good-natured and trusting Madeline wouldn't hear a word against her man. Instead, she accused her friends of being jealous and wanting to destroy her one shot at true love.*

*In the end, Madeline realized her friends were right—pretty soon after "The One" had emptied her checking account, run up her credit cards and left town. How could a smart girl with all that going on suddenly be so . . . stupid?*

---

Some cool new scientific studies show that anatomically it's not such a mystery why a smart girl can be turned into a fool when the love bug bites. Check this out:

Here's your brain:

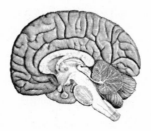

Nice looking pile of noodles there. This 3.5 lb. organ can get your basic modern day hominid through most of her activities of daily living.

Now here is your brain on "love":

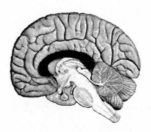

This is a two-dimensional diagram of a brain of someone who's in love. The darker areas approximate the brain region with a huge amount of metabolic activity. This area has more blood flowing to it than the rest of the brain. Funny thing is this "metabolically hot" center sits in an area so primitive that neuroscientists used to call it "the Reptilian Brain." That reptilian brain is responsible for such basic bodily functions as sleeping, waking, and breathing. What's the Romantic Love Center doing all tangled up with that stuff?

According to Anthropologist Helen Fisher[8], the body's chemical signals are what convince you that you're in love, and the effects are much like heroin to a dope fiend. Even their names sound like street drugs: dopamine sounds like dope; epinephrine, whose partial chemical name—methamino-ethyl-benzene—sounds a bit like *methamphetamine*, aka Meth; oxytocin sounds like oxycontin—an opiate with the unfortunate nickname "Hillbilly Heroin."

Meanwhile, when you fall in love, up goes serotonin—one of the brain's natural antidepressants. Prozac became famous for being the first drug to effectively target and raise the level of serotonin. And then there's love, which does the same thing: it keeps your head swimming in serotonin and helps convince you that you're finally, truly happy. How each of the many chemicals contributes to the chain reaction called falling in love is still being studied. But we do know these compounds affect the brain and the heart, causing tension, palpitations, sweating and compulsive thinking. Not to mention an urgent need to snuggle.

This physiologic connection has led anthropologists to suggest that romantic love is not really even an emotion, but rather a biological drive to mate.[9] Imagine a group of early humans—it's likely that the ones who were high on the love drugs would mate more often than those who weren't. In this scenario, Stone Age Girl #1 is experiencing "love."

*Stone Age Girl #1:*
**I think that hairy one is cute.**

*Stone Age Girl #2:*
**No he isn't! Did you see how short his spear is?**

*Stone Age Girl #1:*
**I love that short spear.**
**I don't know why, it just drives me wild!**

Who do you think is more likely to hook up? There's no getting around it, the lustiest early humans would mate most successfully. Our very existence is due to the fact that, smart as we are, we become dumb when we're "in love." No wonder the other basic instincts get put on hold while in pursuit of our "one and only."

These findings about feeling in love were discovered by scanning♥ the brains of hundreds of men and women who claimed to be "in love." Later the researchers rescanned their

---

♥ This scan is performed by a Functional MRI that tracks blood flow and metabolic activity.

subjects when they were "out of love" and found that the Love Center had gone cold.

Now we can find out the answer to one of the most burning questions of all time: How long does romantic love last?

Answer: 18 to 24 months, tops.

Armed with science, no one needs to blame a partner for not being the same "Schnookums" you first met. Your brain simply went back into proper balance and that wondrous biochemical experience that once controlled your every thought either evolved or dissolved.

Case closed.

———— ⚬✕✕⚬ ————

Let's back up here for a minute. We all know what happens when love dissolves—few of us are spared that heartbreak. But what about the love that *evolves* instead?  What about those relationships that *do* stand the test of time? What about that cute couple, married 50 years, who were just caught making out at that wedding last summer?

This is the elusive "happily every after" that we've been trained to expect. It's true that some marriages stay together in seeming bliss for decades. Sure, they may hit wobbly spots here and there, but these couples stick it out—through thick and thin, better, worse, richer, poorer, sickness, whatev. How do they do it?

Conventional wisdom and modern-day media research (okay, Dr. Drew, Dr. Phil and a few episodes of HBO's *Real Sex*) says many of these pairs find ways to at least partially "reignite" the love drug through the years. They each have different and highly personalized formulas. They may prize loyalty, family, religion, the traditions of marriage or perhaps just the positives of being "coupled." Some just really value the other person. And though many may never admit it, they've all felt the urge to walk out and start fresh. Yet these couples hang in there. They aren't chasing the "high" of love, but are experiencing a real partnership. We salute them.

But let's be clear: what these couples *aren't* experiencing, but for some reason it's assumed *they are*, is the magical relationship where the high of the love *drug* never wears off. It doesn't help that most long-term couples are content to have you think they're living the fairytale.

"You can't even understand your own marriage, how are you really going to understand what [other people] are up to?" Susan Squire stated in a Salon.com[10] interview about her book, *I Don't: A Contrarian History of Marriage*. With long lives and long marriages, Squire states, "There are going to be bad times."

Some women accept this. Pamela is happily married with no plans to ever divorce her husband. But after eight years together and two kids, she does not spend her days compulsively checking her voicemail wondering, "Did he call??" as she did during the courtship phase. We all wish we could grab that intoxicating feeling of new love, lock it up and keep it safe. But we can't kid ourselves anymore: Love just doesn't work that way.

### BOTTOM LINE

The latest scientific studies say that "romantic love" is not love at all. It's a thrill that always fades away. Well-invested mutual funds, however, last much longer.

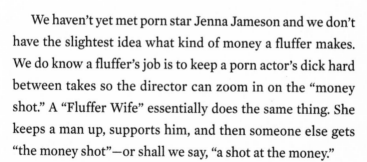

## CHAPTER 5

# The Fluffer Wife

***It serves me right for putting all
my eggs in one bastard.***

DOROTHY PARKER, WRITER

———⟨∞⟩———

We haven't yet met porn star Jenna Jameson and we don't have the slightest idea what kind of money a fluffer makes. We do know a fluffer's job is to keep a porn actor's dick hard between takes so the director can zoom in on the "money shot." A "Fluffer Wife" essentially does the same thing. She keeps a man up, supports him, and then someone else gets "the money shot"—or shall we say, "a shot at the money."

Marrying for love without the slightest concern about the fellow's bank account turns many first wives into glorified fluffers—Fluffer Wives. Let's face it; "security" has nothing to do with feeling secure in someone's arms. You can have that whether you're rich or poor. Security for a man has always been based on money and the status that goes along with it—including a young woman on his arm.

Here's a well-known scenario: a young couple marries for love at 23. She supports him through graduate school and then after a few babies, the love of her life rolls over one morning and says to himself, "Who's this old lady I'm married to?"

Divorce procedures begin. He has a dalliance or two with some secretaries he's been eyeing. He's only forty. But our culture couldn't be more clear—a rich man in his forties is hot. His ex—a 40-year-old divorcée with two toddlers—*not so much.*

In her heart of hearts she can hardly blame him. He traded-up for a younger, sexier woman. She feels old. And that makes her hate him even more.

At 40 he can still get it up. He's pre-Viagra; she's pre-menopausal. He's relaxing in the Jacuzzi with a young hottie; his ex is searching for female lubricant in the drugstore. So now for the awful truth:

### When it comes to marrying well, women have a sell-by date.

So don't be a Fluffer Wife. DO NOT invest in a man's potential at the expense of your own career or fortune hunting. Yes, we realize the occasional gamble can pay off, but let's look at the big picture: We'd love to think our men mean what they say, but NOW we know they don't, or can't. Many think they really, really *will* love you forever—but chances are when he's 40 and making money he won't want you on his arm. The culture rewards him for bailing out. The problem is . . . few gals see what's happening until it's already too late.

Studies have shown that as either partner's fortunes rise dramatically, he or she is apt to start looking for a new mate.[11] With cash comes more confidence, more sex appeal—and more opportunities. The paradox is that if you marry a man with potential, when he finally achieves, he often leaves.

So, girls, beware. Case in point: the true story of Betty Broderick.

## Ripped from the Headlines: A Cautionary Tale

*Betty Broderick was a beauty at 23 when she married her prince. He went to medical and then law school, while Betty worked as a nurse to support them. During these lean years they had four beautiful children.*

*Soon, Dr. Broderick became a medical malpractice attorney. As his financial situation started looking up, he began looking down at the ripe cleavage of his young legal assistant. His temples grayed and he grew more handsome and charismatic, and as he began to amass actual wealth, Betty got the boot.*

*And he moved in with his paramour.*

*Poor Betty felt sorry for herself. As is often typical, the mistress was the spitting image of Betty when she was in her twenties. Betty believed that she was being replaced by a younger version of herself because at the age of 36 she was too "fat and old" (her words).*

*Betty didn't think this was the way her life was supposed to go. She became unhinged. She stalked them, drove her car onto their lawn, and left messages on their answering machine, which included colorful language ("This is a message for fuckhead and the bitch . . . ") and frequent use of the word "cunt."*

*Dr. Broderick sued for divorce and through his connections in the legal community Betty got a mediocre settlement and lost custody of her four children. He and his young, perky wife moved on with their lives.*

*But Betty was stuck on the injustice. This was no fair trade. She had exchanged her youth and her beauty for what she thought would be a lifetime partnership. Betty worked herself up into a self-righteous frenzy. And on an unseasonably warm autumn night she shot her ex-husband and his new wife dead while they lay sleeping in each other's arms.*

*Betty is currently serving a life sentence in the Women's Correctional Institution at Chowchilla.*

Note to Betty: you made the wrong call.

When it comes to divorce, it seems like men have an easy ability to hit the re-start button and grab a new wife and a new life. Meanwhile, the ex-wife, despite often being financially devastated by her divorce, may still secretly mourn the man who dumped her as she approached middle age. Ex-hubby is on vacation in France with nubile secretary while lonely divorcée is in her one-bedroom apartment drinking Chardonnay from a coffee cup and waxing nostalgic about the once great love that her ex-husband has completely forgotten.

Betty is an extreme case. We know someone who had a similar experience, but resisted the urge to commit a major crime.

## Julia and Caesar

*Julia was thrown for a loop when her husband walked out on her and her two young sons after 14 years of marriage. The reason: He didn't love her anymore. His new lover, Candy, sent this e-mail to Julia.*

```
>As Ceaser says, 'Seize the Day!' You can choose
>to be bitter and make a seen, trying to hang on
>to you're broken marriage. Or you can choose to
>go down a more positive track. I'm sure you're
>divorce won't be easy, but you need to come to
>terms with reality.
```

*Julia, age 40, woke up in the middle of the night and reflexively checked her e-mail. She was horrified not only by the woman's inability to spell, but also by her misattribution of the saying, "Carpe Diem." Julia was no Latin scholar, but she felt certain that Julius Caesar never said, "Seize the day." Outraged by Candy's gall, Julia took her husband's mistress's counsel and seized her laptop and forwarded the email to nearly everyone on her mailing list.*

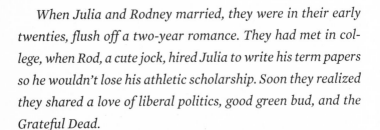

*When Julia and Rodney married, they were in their early twenties, flush off a two-year romance. They had met in college, when Rod, a cute jock, hired Julia to write his term papers so he wouldn't lose his athletic scholarship. Soon they realized they shared a love of liberal politics, good green bud, and the Grateful Dead.*

*Julia quickly fell in love with a man who was equally at home on the playing field or in the kitchen. Julia's intellect, hilarity, and tie-dyed panties brought Rod to his knees.*

*Rod's uncle was a rich investor who treated Rod like his own son. Their wedding was a lavish affair. The young couple happily supported each other in their early careers. But then the marriage took a turn: Rodney set up a bong in the garage and retreated to a pot-addled haze while trying to launch business after failed business.*

*Julia rose through her professional ranks and brought home the bacon. She found out she was expecting their first child, and quit smoking dope. Meanwhile, Rodney came into some cash through his wealthy kin, but put the bulk of it in a separate trust, never intermingling it with the marital money.*

*After 14 years of marriage, when Rodney walked out saying, "You stifle me," Julia was stunned. She had been so busy "having it all" that she hadn't noticed Rodney's change of heart. Like all men, he blamed her. Like all women—she blamed herself.*

*Julia consulted several lawyers. "You may have to pay him alimony," they warned.*

*"But he's rich!" she exclaimed.*

*Julia was surprised to learn that since the family money he received had never been commingled with the marital money, it was all his. And the large inheritance due him down the line was also out of the dispute.*

---

**GOLD-DIGGING ICON QUOTE**

Trust your husband, adore your husband, and get as much as you can in your own name.

*Joan Rivers, Comedian*

*Before Rod even bothered to file for divorce (he waited for Julia to deal with the paperwork) he moved in with twenty-something Candy—and gave her a great job as his "personal assistant."*

In the end, it was young Candy who turned out to be more cunning than the Phi Beta Kappa Julia. Candy traded her youth for cash, while Julia wasted her best years fluffing the same man who broke her home and her heart.

---

**ANTI-FLUFFING QUOTE**

This above all, refuse to be a victim.

*Margaret Atwood, writer*

---

*Not unlike Betty, Julia was overcome with rage and almost lost her mind. She had fantasies of Rod slipping, then falling (in slow motion) down the long brick stairway leading up to the home they once shared. She pictured herself and her sons stoically weeping at Rod's funeral à la Jackie and John-John Kennedy.*

*So very brave . . .*

Many starter wives become aware of their previously undiscovered homicidal tendencies when confronted with a husband's change of heart. Some turn to food, drugs, alcohol or another combination of self-destructive paths. But as Julia's compassionate therapist told her: Get over it. In our culture, if a woman complains of being dumped by her husband, robbed of her "best years" and cast off like yesterday's laundry, she is called a crazy, bitter ex-wife. In the past, society placed the stigma on the cad and tossed him out of his social circles, maybe even his career. These days he's more likely to get a pat on the back and a promotion.

### Julia and Caesar—A Postscript

*After forwarding Candy's e-mail, Julia felt a little better. She went about the business of "seizing the day." This included a full day at work, grocery shopping, a parent-teacher conference, and confirming (by text) to tutor a studly 25-year-old in the art of cunnilingus later that week. Julia was so busy that she had almost forgotten about the Candy-Spam. She was delighted when she came home and found her inbox brimming with responses from around the world.*

*"Couldn't she Google it?" someone replied, "It's not Caesar. It's a Latin poet . . . ." (The e-mail goes on to quote the poem, which is beautiful, but we won't bore you.)*

*"She's an illiterate ignoramus," a friend of Julia's mother wrote.*

*Brainiac Tom typed a single word, "Horace."*

*And on and on. Someone mirthfully mentioned something about croutons and raw eggs, but then it occurred to Julia that her two sons would soon be raised half the week by a nitwit who wouldn't know a Caesar quote from a Caesar salad.*

*And she cried.*

What did Julia do wrong? Her belief in the fairytale marriage blinded her to reality. She thought, especially after the birth of her babies, that marriage was for keeps and the ups and downs went with the territory. Now she was facing middle age alone, with the possibility of having to pay her ex for the privilege of being dumped.

It was Candy, a poster child for gold-digging, who for the time being, came out on top. And although there was no way in hell Candy would ever know it, she had won with Caesar's famous words: "Veni, Vidi, Vici."

**I came. I saw. I conquered.**

———∞∞∞———

But will the conquering hero prevail in the long term? If marriage comes, will Candy be smart enough to avoid becoming "Fluffer #2"? Will she wake up to find an even younger, less-demanding replacement? Is Candy just falling into the same love trap, destined to become another casualty in the mating game? Not if she reads this book.

A rich man with wives numbered one through three is commonplace these days. But being dumped is still heartbreaking, and can lead to loneliness, poverty, homicide, suicide, and more than your fair share of grey hairs and wrinkles.

So beware of marrying potential. Wives who stand by their guys in the lean years may one day remind those men of the struggles they'd sooner forget. So if you decide to throw in your lot with an up-and-comer, remember to work the GDI. In your marriage, *keep an eye on the money* and find your inner bimbo so this doesn't happen to you.

### BOTTOM LINE

Don't fluff.

**CHAPTER 6**

# Farewell: Why We Leave

*I'm not upset about my divorce.*
*I'm just sorry I'm not a widow.*

ROSEANNE BARR, COMEDIAN

You've heard the horror stories, so why do all the most captivating love stories end with the handsome prince marrying the gorgeous princess to live happily ever after? Like the myth of love, it turns out this one-liner is just another punchline in one of life's better (bitter?) jokes.

### GOLD-DIGGING GIRL FACT

50% of all first time marriages fail

75% of second marriages fail

*US Census Bureau, 2000*

It's an established fact that approximately half of all marriages end in divorce. A survey by AOL and *Woman's Day Magazine* found that one out of three of those that stay married said they would NOT marry their husbands again, and 20% more said they weren't *sure* if they would.[12]

So of all those that stay married, half of them are miserable, and the other half either have marriages that work *or* they are lying about it. So 25% or *less* of all marriages are really happily ever after and have the kind of golden partnerships that dreams are made of. Bottom line: Less than 25% of all marriages work.

## Percent of All Marriages

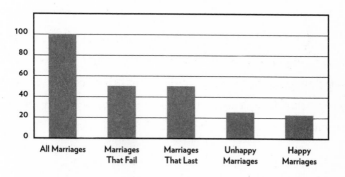

*Data from AOL/Woman's Day Magazine Survey*

None of this is really news. Right? Then why do we act surprised and appalled when we hear about adultery and subsequent divorce? The statistics put the truth to the lie of fidelity. We're not really all dogs, we're human—which, if you really think about it, comes with a lot more opportunity for vice and deceit.

And what about the issue of how marriage plays out in other cultures? In some countries couples are divorced 10 times and think it's perfectly normal.[13] Perhaps it's time to get over our preoccupation with lifelong monogamous partnership.

We mentioned wolves as one of the few animal species that mate for life, but even *they* still have sex with other wolves on the side. Many bird species pair up for chick-rearing purposes, but it seems humans are the only species that attempt the crap shoot of fidelity—*and* go to pieces when someone cheats.

We have the facts—so why do we break our own hearts when it doesn't work out?

―――⚬∞∞⚬―――

## Half of Us

*Becky adored Kevin, a charmer who wrote poetry but had no real career ambitions. They were sweethearts in college, then after graduation, Becky received an offer to work for a couture fashion house in France. While she was abroad, Kevin went to bed with a girl or two, but missed Becky terribly. Suddenly he found that he couldn't live without her.*

Meanwhile, Becky (now going by "Becca") had a taste of some French men for herself. She couldn't resist it when she walked down the streets in Paris and men stepped up off the curb onto their doorsteps, looked her in the eye and said "Enchante." This never happened back in Chicago. Her French got better, she dressed differently and her foreignness made her irresistible to some Parisian guys. She was a happy (and well-satisfied) American in Paris.

Then one day, Kevin crossed the ocean to profess his undying love. "Come home and be mine forever," he begged. He promised the sun, the moon and the stars. Paris was great, mused Becca, but it didn't compare with a lifetime of traveling a galaxy of love with her celestial soul mate. She returned to the Windy City. They set a date, got married, and had two children soon after.

Four years later at the tender age of 28, Becky (who had dropped her sexier nickname) noticed that the magic had somehow vanished. Her life seemed a blur of bottles and dirty diapers, and soon she could no longer squeeze into her "fat jeans." She felt bloated and trapped. Her once promising future had vanished when she set aside her career to be a stay-at-home mom.

Kevin suffered as well. He struggled with the bills. The monotony of being a family man bored him. He hooked up with a girl at his office—and oops—got caught.

*After bitter recriminations, the two split. Kevin quickly remarried and started a new family, leaving Becky broke, broken, and totally bewildered.*

Well, she shouldn't be. It's textbook. Most marriages end when folks are in their twenties, about two to four years in, and often—about 30% to 50% of the time—with young children in the house.[14] The good news is if you have five or more children the divorce rate drops to near zero. You might want to try that one if you're determined to hang on.

Again we must ask, what went wrong? Here we turn again to anthropology and the work of David M. Buss and Helen Fisher, PhD, in order to get some perspective on this issue of mating so we can stop the whole shock-and-awe routine when we walk out on each other.

Meet our Adam and Eve.

See how they are standing upright? They hunt and gather in the open plains and are at high risk from attack by hungry predators. When we went bipedal, small children could no longer ride on mom's back. She had to carry the little rascals in her arms and couldn't put them down to help with the work, lest she risk dire consequences.

*Child: "Ooh, look at nice kitty."*

*Saber-toothed tiger: "Thanks for dinner."*

So "going bipedal" forced humanoid females to become dependent on their mates for food, protection and other resources for the first time in history. The females carried their babes in their arms until the age of reason—about four or five years. This would be at about the time that a man's responsibilities to a particular woman would have ended. Hmmm. That's the same time frame in which most modern marriages tank.

Anthropologists theorize that in pre-historic cultures, after discharging his responsibilities to his Baby-Mama, the man wouldn't have been viewed as a lout by the other proto-humans when he abandoned her and took up with someone else. Like the modern-day man who "marries up," he would maintain a decent social status within the group.[15] By the way, she too may have begun to look elsewhere after having been disappointed by him in some way. (Perhaps the toothpaste cap . . . it's anyone's guess.) But no one in the social order would mind because the survival of the group was the most important issue.

Now anecdotally it seems that men are the ones doing most of the ditching, but in reality *both* sexes stray. We've all known men to be devastated, though most times only briefly, by an errant wife. It turns out, Helen Fisher suggests, that the person who feels powerful in the relationship is usually the one to walk. This may help explain why battered partners often don't leave their abusers. More and more often, it's the women who do the leaving. Here's a story from the heartland.

## Moving On Up

*Sherry and Jeremy grew up in a small town in Iowa. They married right after high school graduation. He was a tall, handsome sweetheart of a guy. At Sherry's urging, they left their tiny hometown so he could seek his fortune in Des Moines.*

*Jeremy's Midwest upbringing made him simple, honest, and kind. He only had small town aspirations, but together they made the move. He worked in construction and earned a decent income. He designed and hand-built a stunning, one-of-a-kind home for his beloved wife and soon they had a baby.*

*As time passed, Sherry grew bored with life at home. She was itching to get out and about. Sure, Jeremy was a babe (and hot in the sack), but she yearned for more. She thought a second paycheck might do the trick, so she got a low-level job in state government and soon was spending more and more nights out on the town—dressed up at fundraisers and other political functions. Jeremy hammered away at work and stayed home to watch their son, while she was out meeting many high rollers with coffers and connections.*

*Here was Sherry, this peach-faced gal from the heartland, looking great in high heels while earnestly trying to make a difference in the world we live in. What could have made a cynical politician pop a bone faster than that?*

*She left Jeremy for one of these rich men. She called up to her soon-to-be ex-husband from their front yard—announcing her departure while he was nailing shingles on the roof of their home.*

*She wanted more—much more— and though she had loved Jeremy from the age of 16, it wasn't until she was a little older and smarter that she realized that love wasn't enough for her. It wasn't even close.*

*Ultimately, Sherry had no regrets. She moved to Washington D.C. and became a model political wife. And Jeremy? He was left broken-hearted and angry. He threw himself into his work and wound up accidentally cutting off a finger in a pique of rage.*

Is it just us or has the promise, "Until death do us part" lost all meaning? It's become a bigger lie than when a guy, overcome with passion, whispers in a girl's ear, "I swear, babe, I'll only put it in a little bit!"

———⊙⊙⊙———

Let's check back in with our Adam and Eve. Congrats! Baby on the way!

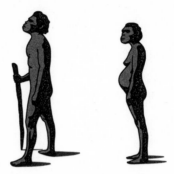

With a life expectancy of maybe 40, these creatures were astonishingly vulnerable to their environment. When a man hunted he could get injured or killed. He could prove himself inept as a provider. He could disgrace himself in some way and be viewed with disdain by his mate who would be wise to look elsewhere for her provisions.

What about her? She was likely to be injured in childbirth and succumb to death. She could prove herself to be a poor caretaker to their children or fail at the fine art of foraging.

With both parties at high risk for decline in social status, disease, and death, the most evolutionarily adaptive response to these precarious circumstances would be to maintain a watchful eye for alternative mates in the group. That is—if your genes were to survive.

Those of us who are alive today are descendents of those who wisely shifted alliances and bedmates when it was prudent to do so. Truth be told, we're living in modern times with bodies equipped for a Stone Age world. In some ways we're evolved, but our bodies betray our ape-like tendencies. Take, for example, the goose bumps that pop up on your arms when you get cold. The reaction is meant to raise your body hair to keep in heat. Notice how it doesn't warm you up? It's another leftover response designed for bodies covered in fur. (That one guy in college you called "The Missing Link" doesn't count—he's waxing his back these days.)

An effective flight-or-fight response boosted the chance of survival for those living on open savannahs. Our ancestors really had no other options. We still experience that panic when we feel threatened, though many spend more money than they should on therapists to work through it. It turns out we really should go ahead and blame our parents—or maybe ancient ancestors—and invest the therapy money in an interest-bearing account instead.

It's easy to see that our bodies and our instincts are downright pre-historic. Nevertheless, the demands we place on the modern marriage are more exacting than ever, designed for an idealized modern human. There's an obvious paradox. So let's not be surprised by being abandoned or by jumping ship ourselves. Turns out we all carry deep inside us a scoundrel's heart.

Taking all of this into account then, how can we guarantee a long-lasting marriage? Anthropologist David Buss[16] offers the following:

> ***To preserve a marriage couples should remain faithful; produce children together; have ample economic resources; be kind, generous, and understanding; and never refuse or neglect a mate sexually.***

Good luck with all that! Despite our best intentions, all couples encounter scads of difficulties as they attempt to attain these ideals. After all, people change, get bored, turn out to be sterile, lose their jobs, develop far-out tastes, fall out of love, stop wanting sex . . . And these are just a few of the many reasons to end the modern marriage. We could go on. And we will. But for now, stop being conned: for most people "happily ever after" is just another fairytale ending that never really comes true.

## BOTTOM LINE

Economic resources never get angry, ask if you've gained weight, or forget to call home.

## CHAPTER 7

# Fight the Fantasy

**Just say no.**

Romantic love may feel magical, but it's not magic. It is, however, a one-of-a-kind experience and we know you want it. We all do . . . even those of us who have been burned time and time again continue to chase the dragon.

Our passions can overwhelm us, drive us mad, make us dumb, and result in herpes. Love's a bitch, everybody has always known that. Thanks to the work of marriage historian Stephanie Coontz, we also know how other cultures have viewed romantic love. In many parts of India, falling in love without marrying first is still considered disruptive and anti-social. The ancient Greeks thought love to be a form of insanity. In the Middle Ages, the French called love a "derangement of the mind curable through intercourse." In dynastic China, the pesky rush of emotion was viewed as a threat to the solidarity of the family.

In much of the world most of the time, romantic love was considered too temporary an emotion upon which to build a life together. These days it's considered the only truly moral basis to build a life together. Rather than pursuing love, we suggest pursuing a lifestyle with a man you like, or admire or enjoy. But in any case, he should be a man with resources.

Throughout history, many a marriage entered into for practical means evolved into long, fulfilling unions, while many a "love match" ended in a bitter dissolution. Henry the Eighth was passionately in love with Anne Boleyn for years while he was still married to his first wife Katherine of Aragon, whom he could not divorce under the Church's law. Driven by his ardor for Anne, Henry severed age old ties to the head of the Vatican and created a new English church in order to make Anne his Queen. Three years after their wedding, Henry found he'd fallen out of love with Boleyn, so he severed Anne's head from her body and announced his engagement to another girl the following day. They were married within a fortnight.♥

So don't lose your head; at least modern divorce is a little less painful than public execution. With 50-50 odds of keep-

---

♥ One day after Anne's execution in 1536, King Henry became engaged to Jane Seymour. They were married 10 days later. www.wikipedia.org. Accessed 10/29/08.

ing a marriage intact, love alone is not a good enough reason to head down the aisle.

———— ⚭ ————

To support our case, we have decided to include the results of our own intensive analysis of romantic love:

LOVE is a PRIMITIVE INSTINCT.

❤

LOVE is a BIOCHEMICAL RESPONSE.

❤

LOVE is an ADDICTION.

❤

LOVE DOESN'T LAST.

❤

## BOTTOM LINE

See above.

## CHAPTER 8

# Fragments: X & Y

*Why can't a woman be more like a man?*

HENRY HIGGINS, MY FAIR LADY

## Smart Girl's Science Lesson

As we researched the material for this book, we began to look closely at the differences between men and women. We looked so damn close we ended up at the microscopic level where we found that every cell in our bodies is fundamentally different, right down to our chromosomes.

A chromosome is a bundle of DNA— it contains the genes that make us who we are. Chromosomes don't travel alone; they're paired up, and most people have 23 sets of these little duos in each cell. One of these pairings, the "XY" match-up, is the one that determines if the baby will be a boy. "XX" and you get a baby girl.

The X and Y chromosomes are so named because under the microscope, they supposedly look like the letters "X" and "Y." To begin, let's take a look at these two letters of the alphabet to see why *one of these things is not like the other*.

X and Y. It's the genetic difference between men and women. Notice anything missing? Let's take another look:

Now whether you're a Harvard graduate or never finished high school—if you just keep looking, you'll see that something has gone terribly wrong. From where we're sitting, it appears that *at least 25%* of the essential information is missing from a man's Y chromosome.

Now 25% off may seem like a bargain at a department store sale, but sometimes you end up bringing home something you don't even need—or really want. And when it comes to men, we *deplore* bargain shopping.

Now let's go a step further and look at a microscopic view of the XY pairing:

In reality, the X (pictured on the left) is three times as long as the puny Y. Doesn't it look like the runt of the litter? That's because it is—teeny tiny Y carries only a few dozen genes, compared to big momma X, who is packing 1500. Apparently the Y has been shrinking—and at this point has lost almost all of its original genes. The Y chromosome that boys inherit nowadays is but a shadow of its former self. In addition, it contains old, rotten relic genes that don't do *anything*—which makes scientists think the decay is still going on.

This isn't to say that men are rotting from the inside out (although in some circles that's debatable). Throughout the evolutionary process, genes are swapped around, but in the case of the Y, there is no exchange, and it looks like it's just getting smaller. Genes on the X chromosomes are many and continually varied; an argument could be made that X chromosomes are like oversized women's purses—loaded with things we don't need or can't find.

But from our point of view, a person might feel a bit sorry for the Y chromosome and its evolutionary disintegration. After all, with so much genetic information missing, it's a wonder men can walk around on their own, the poor dears. But they do, and how wonderful they look with their broad shoulders, their confident gait, striding across the playing field covered in sweat, through the workplace to their corner offices or across the stage to the podiums accepting awards for their fabulousness.

We love men.

But we're not like them.

Men turn us on. They fight for our honor; they take out the garbage, lift heavy objects and occasionally give us orgasms. But it's clear that guys and gals are so different it's no wonder we have problems communicating. But then again, much of the time, we actually don't. Take for example, Adam and Eve—these days they go by the names Sharon and Ted.

*Sharon and Ted are on their first date. She is practiced in the art of flirting: how to bend her neck, look up at her man admiringly and dumb down her conversation.*

*She muses, "I wonder if he's getting to like me. He seems to be leaning in toward me. His foot is touching mine. That's a sure sign of interest. He's so handsome and successful. He could be Mr. Right."*

*On the other hand, Ted thinks, "I can't believe it; I think I can see her nipple through her shirt. I bet I'm going to fuck her tonight!"*

Most of us already know that men and women often seem to live in parallel universes, and although it might look like they are sharing a moment together, each may be having a completely different experience. This extends to all areas of life, not just dating. The work environment, especially, emphasizes our ability to coexist in the exact same environments while having very different perspectives.

———— ∞ ————

Another thing worth repeating is that men only get one Y chromosome. Women, on the other hand, get two X chromosomes. These X's pair up and tango with each other, swapping genetic information in a process that ultimately leads to evolution of the species.

At some point back in time, the Y was able to boogie too, swapping genes just as well as the next chromosome. But over the eons, for some reason, the Y dropped out of the dance and started getting smaller and smaller.

Just look at him now, bless his little heart.

The end result is that these fragments, the Y's, pass down from generation to generation completely unaltered and un-evolved.

For crying out loud, according to the *American Journal of Human Genetics*, an estimated 16 MILLION men are walking around on earth today with the EXACT same Y chromosome that Genghis Kahn was walking around with 1,000 years ago! So when men claim that they are primitive cave dwellers, believe them.

## BOTTOM LINE

Less than 1% genetic difference between men and women makes all the difference in the world.

**CHAPTER 9**

# Faux Pas—Sex and the Workplace

### *I did not have sexual relations with that woman.*

PRESIDENT BILL CLINTON

You may think you can take refuge from the mating game while pursuing your career. But our genetic differences play out everywhere—especially at work—and they can interfere with even the smartest girl's plans.

Nowadays it's common to spend our best waking hours in the workplace, leaving the exhausted fringes of the day for family and friends. Recent studies have shown that our "turbo-capitalism" makes 60-hour weeks the norm in many work environments, and we take pride in the number of hours we labor.

Colleague #1: "I worked 58 hours this week on the project!"

Colleague #2: "Oh yeah, well I'm missing my sister's wedding because I have to work through the weekend."

Colleague #3: "That's nothing, I took a conference call during my triple bypass last month."

With all the time spent together, workmates can become closer than family and social interactions are often work-related. "Who wants to walk over to the bar after we wrap this up?" is the family motto.

It's no wonder the workplace becomes a single's dating pool. All those hours spent together create automatic intimacy. We gripe about office politics and joke with one another to break tension. Office attractions, romances and affairs bubble up out of those shared moments of dissatisfaction and the experience of creating projects side-by-side.

Despite all the long hours, the physical closeness, the kidding around and the out-and-out flirting, pretty much everyone likes to think, "I'm not the type to let something like that happen at work." Both men and women make these declarations, ignoring the fact that sexuality infuses the room like a nerve gas and gives our brains invisible and often irresistible instructions.

## Medical Malpractice

*Carolina was a hard-as-nails third year resident in Medi-
cine at a large hospital in the Northeast when she began her
month as "ER Chief." She was scheduled every other night to
work with Antonio, a handsome ER resident from Spain, who
was new to the hospital.*

*The first time she saw him, he nodded and said, "Buenos
dias, Guapa." Carolina thought he was cute, so she ran to her
office to Google "guapa."*

*The next time she saw him, she wasn't as impressed. He was
standing over a bleeding trauma patient and he seemed over-
whelmed. Antonio stood aloof doing nothing, while the nurses
were cutting off the patient's clothes and struggling to get intra-
venous access. Carolina's only thoughts were of the patient as
she hurried to assist.*

*"We can't get access," one of the nurses said as she looked to
Antonio for help. He stepped forward to put in a central line,
but failed twice.*

*Carolina gently nudged him aside, softly saying, "Let me give
it a try." She easily slid the catheter deep into the blue lumen of
the jugular vein, placing the tip right next to the entrance of the
patient's beating heart. Antonio said nothing but his eyes com-
municated thanks and admiration for her skills.*

*A few shifts and about eight Code Blues later, they found
themselves sharing coffee on the hospital's rooftop helipad. As*

*she strained to understand his thick Spanish accent, what began as an innocent conversation about technique under pressure slowly morphed into what felt like a date. Staring into her coffee cup, she fantasized about him taking her in his arms to share a passionate kiss worthy of a movie scene with George Clooney.*

*By the third week Carolina was heady from the pheromones rising off their skin as they sweated together over patients— some living, others dying. Her heart leapt when she saw him. She tried to hide her joy at his proximity, even the little thrill she felt when their hands so much as brushed over a patient. But she was sure nothing would happen—her life was no soap opera.*

*Then one day Carolina was checking on a comatose patient when Antonio pushed open the curtain and closed it behind him. It was against all kinds of codes of professional conduct, but the sexual tension was too much for either of them to withstand. He pushed her up against the beeping EKG monitor, grabbed her face and kissed her deep and hard.*

*Within a couple of days, they found themselves on Antonio's futon having athletic sex under his annoyingly bright skylight. Soon, for Carolina their relationship began to feel like something special. Over the next two weeks, it seemed Antonio woke up at Carolina's place nearly as often as his own. Carolina let her mind run wild with dreams of a romantic future with Antonio and she realized she couldn't deny it anymore: She was in love.*

*Not so with Antonio. He kept his romantic murmurings to lines like "I love making love to you." He was already looking elsewhere. Carolina was another notch on his well-notched futon post. But she didn't realize the truth until he asked her one day, "Who's that little mousy intern?"*

*Carolina looked over and saw a plain girl. Nothing special.*

*While Carolina shrugged, Antonio said with his thick Spanish accent, "I like that leettle mouse."*

*And Carolina's heart began to break.*

---

Besides the fact that Antonio was a Don Juan of the highest caliber, other elements were at play here. Although Antonio admitted that he loved Carolina's hot tight body and that her strengths as ER Chief were admirable qualities, ultimately he wasn't deeply attracted. On the other hand, he and the mouse stayed together for years.

These days, sexual intercourse can be as meaningless as a handshake. But all of us girls know that once we're penetrated, the bolts that lock the vault to our hearts can begin to turn. The physiological changes that occur during a sexual affair can wreak havoc on the most professional among us. "Love" or what we perceive to be love, can cause the most intelligent and well-behaved women (and men) to act like complete jackasses. So we need to be careful.

Anecdotally, this sex-at-work thing seems to be harder for women than for men. The married guy who cheats can often get away with it after the tearful *I-never-meant-for-it-to-happen* confession. His co-workers smile knowingly, and somehow his reputation is slightly enhanced. Though some of the girls in the office brand him an SOB, there's oftentimes no real negative affect to his productivity or job security.

Meanwhile, the object of his short-lived passion is dealt a different hand of cards. As the town whore, she is left in a far more vulnerable position. She may be ostracized, whispered about, referred to as the office joke and, in the worse case scenario, fired. If she does manage to keep her job, she may end up quitting because the mean-spirited gossip and open hostility make the workplace intolerable.

And even if you're cautious and professional and avoid workplace liaisons at all costs, you can still get screwed. It will be a surprise to some and old news to many that the "casting couch" still exists. And it's challenging for a "victim" to prove her harassment claims in court unless "Mr. Hands" is straightforward, usually vulgar, and witnessed by others. And even more annoying: Women can be penalized in the workplace even if they *do not* engage in sex with a boss. He may find ways to punish her out of spite. And what happens if she accepts them? It can go either way. Carolina got an unexpected bonus when she indulged in yet another office liaison.

## More Medical Malpractice

*Carolina's memories of Antonio faded with her transfer to the Medical ICU. There she worked with the Chief of Critical Care, an angry, demanding boss who was notorious for throwing scalpels at interns during morning rounds. He took a special liking to the fit and pretty Carolina, and he propositioned her constantly, though he was careful to make sure no other staff member was nearby.*

*For a moment Carolina actually considered the question, "Can a nice girl still fuck her way to the top?"*

*Chief Franks was nationally prominent and it wouldn't hurt her career to have him on her side. But compared to Antonio he was bestial—wrinkled with long tufts of white hair protruding from his nostrils and ears. He looked decrepit, despite his somewhat stylish choice of a high quality diamond stud in his left ear . . . tuft adjacent. But Carolina had already had enough of workplace liaisons and rebuffed Chief Franks' often inappropriate advances.*

*Carolina thought she was handling the situation properly. Then she heard a rumor that Chief Franks was infuriated that Carolina had an affair with a mere resident, but not with him.*

She considered that perhaps her broken heart led her to make a mistake in rejecting Franks.

And after all, she thought, "I could use some adoration after being kicked to the curb." One late night, Carolina was determined to set things straight. She went to Franks' office dressed only in her white coat and a lacy, pearled thong. This was daring and she was scared. When he saw her, Franks seemed pissed.

She stuttered something about a bicarb drip in bed seven. He berated her for bothering him when he was trying to finish a research paper. Her face flushed. She apologized. She turned to leave, and with her nerves jangling she dropped her Blackberry. She was almost in tears. She got down on her hands and knees to pick up the pieces of the gadget she didn't have the money to replace.

She'd forgotten about her panties, but Franks caught a glimpse of them. He leaned down to help her pick up the broken PDA. After an hour of moaning and groaning that could be heard through the halls and down the elevator shaft, Carolina only emerged from his office when the nurses called a Code Blue on bed seven.

Chief Franks turned out to be an ardent and skillful lover and became a loyal friend. He helped Carolina land the fellowship of her choice and continued to pull strings for her throughout her career. These days she wears her hair in an austere style. Except for those who heard their raucous office sex romps, today no *one would ever guess that a pair of pearled panties had helped secure her position at the top.*

In this case, everything worked out well. Sure, Carolina nursed a broken heart. But who hasn't? She went back to work and used all her assets. Maybe if she hadn't slept with Chief Franks things would have turned out differently. She'd heard rumors about other girls whose careers he'd badly damaged. But she seldom thinks about it now and counts him among her dearest friends. She never married, but became one of the top docs in her field.

### BOTTOM LINE

Sex in the workplace can be dangerous.
If you must indulge, choose your partners
carefully… and don't get screwed.

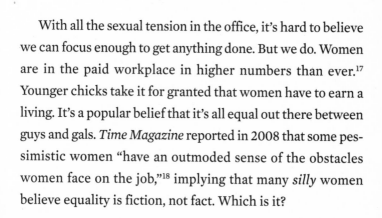

CHAPTER 10

# Fooled: The Myth of Meritocracy

*When I'm with men in the studio, they don't like a woman telling them what to do, no matter how famous you are.*

SHAKIRA, ROCKSTAR

With all the sexual tension in the office, it's hard to believe we can focus enough to get anything done. But we do. Women are in the paid workplace in higher numbers than ever.[17] Younger chicks take it for granted that women have to earn a living. It's a popular belief that it's all equal out there between guys and gals. *Time Magazine* reported in 2008 that some pessimistic women "have an outmoded sense of the obstacles women face on the job,"[18] implying that many *silly* women believe equality is fiction, not fact. Which is it?

## Carly's Folly

*Back in 1999, Carly Fiorina became the first female CEO of a Fortune 20 corporation. As the head of Hewlett Packard, she was named the most powerful woman in business by Fortune Magazine for five years running. She was held up as proof that the workplace was now a true meritocracy.*

*"The executive ranks have accepted a woman," young business women thought. "It's no longer the land of the Big Swinging Dicks!"*

*But in 2005, after a clash with the board, Ms. Fiorina—a classic business pin-up girl—was publicly fired. Business magazines went wild for the story and filled pages with speculation. Had hiring a woman CEO been no more than an HP publicity stunt? Can women handle the stress? Maybe there was something wrong with her! Or had she failed spectacularly on so many levels that it was impossible to know where to begin? No one knew all the details, but everyone had a point of view (and you can buy Carly's book to get her side of the story).*

*Despite her humiliating dismissal, Carly left with a reported $21 million dollar severance package and managed somehow to cobble together a life. But while she was at HP, she was a legend. Although not an entrepreneur, in the business world she had become almost as recognizable a brand as Donald Trump or Martha Stewart.*

*For girls wearing their first business suits, she was living proof that women could make it to the top. Thanks to Carly, they thought the only thing standing between a hard-working smart girl and success were the shattered shards left behind when she busted through the glass ceiling.*

Carly's story may seem like ancient history, but it offers a lesson relevant for today's smart girl. As a pin-up girl, Carly was a token—the exception that's supposed to prove that all the rules had changed. She was quickly replaced by a man and the situation for executive women isn't all that different from the way it was before Carly's shining moment. It's still challenging for a girl to make it to the tip top, no matter how competent. Like the myth of Cinderella and true love, the myth of equality in the workplace needs to be examined.

Consider that in the top accounting firms 50% of new hires are women, yet only 10% achieve partnership. Who are the 90% that achieve partnership? You guessed it. They have penises. The same guys who are kicking us out of our bedrooms as we pass 40 are the same ones squeezing us out of the boardrooms as we approach middle age.

Look, we're not saying progress hasn't been made for working women. We know there are women who have sky-rocketing careers in a wide range of professions. Millionaire author and porn entrepreneur Jenna Jameson writes, produces and stars in her own films. Paper-recycling billionaire Zhang Yin is the richest self-made woman in the world. J.K. Rowling wrote a book while on welfare and is now swimming in dough. We love *all twelve* of the women CEOs in the Fortune 500 (Go Angela! Go Indra!).

We admire influential women like Oprah, Hillary, Condoleeza, Ruth Bader Ginsburg, Joycelyn Elders and Antonia Novella♥... but statistically, there aren't as many as there should be.

---

### GOLD-DIGGING QUOTE

Out of 126 medical schools in the US, only 11 have female deans.

*New England Journal of Medicine*

---

But for the rest of us, dare we risk the most of us— in the more than 40 years since we started toward the land of economic equality we gals just haven't come far enough or fast enough. We know it's important to take the long view of things, but as we've heard said, in the long view, we'll all be dead. Sacrifice is a time-honored tradition, but it's taking too much time. Women's lives matter now.

---

♥ Oprah Winfrey (Queen of All Media), Hilary Clinton (Secretary of State), Condoleeza Rice (former Secretary of State) Ruth Bader Ginsburg (Supreme Court Justice), Joycelyn Elders (first female Surgeon General), Antonia Novella (first female Hispanic Surgeon General)

# Workplace Realities

Just to give you an idea of where women stand in relation to their male counterparts, let's look at some statistics in some everyday careers.

## *Gender Percentages at Entry-Level and Top-Level Jobs*

| Careers | New Hires | Women Power Players | The Real Power Players |
|---|---|---|---|
| Accounting | 50% women | 10% of partners are women | 90% men |
| Law | >50% women | 7% of equity partners are women | 93% men |
| Biological Sciences | 50% women | Less than 10% of science professors are women | More than 90% men |
| Medicine | 50% women | Less than 5% chiefs of departments are women | More than 95% men |

These stats garnered from *The Price of Motherhood* were summed up by author Ann Crittenden this way: "Buried in these numbers are a lot of abandoned dreams." Not the Cinderella dream, but the "I can do it on my own" dream. We all believe it when we're starting out. And why shouldn't we? We saw it on *Oprah*.

But look at the numbers one more time. Are women equal to men in the workplace, or are we still all workin' for the *man*? See the table above and decide for yourself.

In fact, given the current conditions, we think one of the only reasons to get anywhere near the glass ceiling is to take a good look at which executive you plan to score.

## Pay Dirt

As mentioned, of the 500 CEOs who sit at the top of the financial heap, 488 are men and 12 are women. So we know that women aren't exactly making it in the executive ranks. When passed over for promotion by Tom, Dick or Harry, a gal often hears, "It's just not the right fit."

That's not surprising since the suit she has to wear is a tailored Armani 40-Tall.

On the whole, girls are relegated to lower paying jobs and over our lifetimes we lose a fortune due to job transitions and family responsibilities. The Institute for Women's Policy Research says that between the ages of 25 and 60, a woman earns $225,000 while a man hauls in $750,000. Here's the math:

## A Man's Lifetime Salary =
## A Woman's Lifetime Salary x 3

"Why even fucking bother?" one might cheerfully ask. Well, we have to bother because the long-term low income earners are 90% women. You may be tempted to think, "Who cares? That doesn't apply to me." But you'd happen to be dead wrong.

### GOLD-DIGGING GIRL FACT

"Women with bachelor's degrees earn less than men with only a high school diploma or less."

*National Committee on Pay Equity, 2006*

Marriage to just any ol' guy will save our butts for a while: The average married woman's standard of living lags only a little behind that of men. But if the marriage crashes, it's the women who are exposed to an extremely high risk of poverty. Why? Because on average married women make half what their husbands earn. Women contribute to the family in other valuable ways, which are often not compensated—especially after the union is dissolved. On the other hand, men generally continue on without enormous economic consequence, whether they stay married or not.

> ### GOLD-DIGGING QUIP
>
> I'll never marry again. I'm just going to find a woman I hate and buy her a house.
>
> *Rod Stewart, Pop Star*

The data are clear: If you depend on your career, and then marry *just* for love with no concern for your spouse's ability to earn, you're very likely to end up abandoned *and* broke.

Knowing all this, shouldn't we smart girls take a different tack?

## The Worst Case Scenario

In case we're still not getting through to you, let's carry this scenario all the way out. It's hard because none of us likes to think about getting old. But if we live long enough, most of us ladies will retire without a pension and alone, no longer married even if we had once tied the knot. So once again, we can't count on Jack, because he was nimble and he was quick and he ran off with the girl, thin as a candlestick.

What does this all mean? One out of every five elderly women who is alone at retirement will be living *below the poverty level.*[19] Alone, wrinkled and broke? It doesn't sound like a very good deal to us.

### BOTTOM LINE

Despite all the fairy tales and pin-up girls, the establishment still insists on keeping the top jobs and the best goodies for the boys.

### CHAPTER 11

# Fast-Track: Be a Man

***Some of us are becoming the men
we wanted to marry.***

GLORIA STEINEM, FEMINIST ICON

As we smart gals try to get ahead at work, even the most successful among us will admit that it's pretty much a man's world. In fact a recent Harvard Women's Law Association Guidebook encouraged women to "act like men" in order to thrive.

As women, we know that we *can* have great careers—we know that we're every bit as capable as the next guy. But even without going to Harvard Law most of us know the most expedient way to climb the ladder is to act like a guy. So far it's the best way to survive in our competitive work environment. Yet for most of us, it's enough to bring tears to our eyes.

## The Ladies' Room

*Maura was so angry with her boss she was sobbing in the bathroom. Lydia from the law firm upstairs had just finished a good cry and was reapplying makeup.*

*"I hate that man!" Maura choked.*

*Lydia looked at her with only a hint of compassion. "You're the one who wanted to be an investment banker. You'll just cry until you get your paycheck."*

*Maura tried to smile as she splashed water on her face.*

*The bathroom itself was large and adorned with rose-colored granite flecked with black: feminine but strong. Throughout most of the day the stalls and sinks echoed with the tears of a revolving series of weeping women from the investment banks, private equity firms, law partnership, consulting companies and even a tiny graphic design firm that shared the top three floors.*

*Lydia asked, "Do you need Visine?"*

*Maura nodded and Lydia handed her a fresh bottle, "Well, when you're done at the wailing wall use this. But I need it back."*

*The women may not have all known each other, but they did know that in order to survive at work tears were top secret.*

Kimberly Elsbach, a specialist in organizational behavior, has explored the professional consequences of crying.[20] She says working women spend a significant amount of time and effort hiding tears on the job. "Men typically don't cry as often as women and don't have to spend as much energy working to suppress tears on the job," says Elsbach. "It's an enormous burden women have that men don't."

Previous research has found that across cultures women are more likely than men to cry due to frustration, stress, anger, or in response to criticism. In Elsbach's study, every woman she interviewed had cried at work at least once and most said they had to hide it. We know a gal who is constantly claiming to suffer from terrible environmental allergies in order to mask her reactions to workplace stress. Our favorite story was when our friend Grace pretended to have witnessed a horrible traffic accident on Sunset Blvd. when in truth she had just received the worst performance review of her career.

All working gals know that stuffing down emotions helps maintain credibility in the short term. But denying our natural compassion can be costly, not only to the individual but to the workplace as a whole. Why? Because in addition to being big crybabies, we gals have an enormous ability to empathize with others who need help or guidance.

## The Cost of Compassion

*Jane, who works for a large car loan company, recently received criticism from her boss, who said she was "too compassionate" with her direct reports. One of her employees had just suffered the loss of his wife to cancer and another was pregnant, so Jane was juggling their assignments to make sure they were able to attend to their families. Jane thought she would be praised rather than criticized for managing these problems.*

*As her boss delivered his verdict on Jane's disregard for company policy, she stood up to her male supervisor and insisted that her empathy would create loyalty from her people and retain them in the long term. "I will not," she said, "be a dick about this."*

*Luckily, in Jane's case, she didn't get fired on the spot. But she is feeling paranoid. She fears she should have acted like a man, taken the feedback, and kept her mouth shut.*

In the movie version of this story, Jane would lose her job and then be vindicated in the end for doing the right thing. As of now, the verdict on Jane has yet to be delivered. She may yet be fired or managed out. Nevertheless, she's still proud that she stood up for who she is: a considerate manager who believes in her policies. Let's face it, compassion is scarce these days and we need it.

If women can bring compassion to public policy, studies show, they can have an impact that counts. Although American women weren't even allowed to vote (much less hold public office) until 1920, since then we've had a massive impact. When gals bring their yin to the yang of male-dominated government, shit happens. Several studies demonstrate that when more females sit in state legislature, more bills are passed that safeguard women, children, families, and the infirm.[21] In other words, with women in the loop, the public agenda changes to encompass the whole population—men included.

Perhaps one day the "be a man" strategy will be a thing of the past. When that will happen, and how, is anybody's guess. But it's definitely not happening today . . . or tomorrow. In the meantime, the entire pretense is a tough act to keep up.

## BOTTOM LINE

It may just be better for your health and
your wealth to *marry* a man than to act like one.

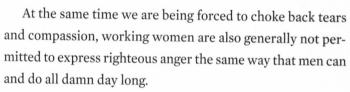

# CHAPTER 12

# Furious: Anger at Work

**You shall know the truth, and the truth shall make you mad.**

ALDOUS HUXLEY, AUTHOR

At the same time we are being forced to choke back tears and compassion, working women are also generally not permitted to express righteous anger the same way that men can and do all damn day long.

Older studies have found that showing anger at work can strengthen your image. After all, displaying anger shows dominance over others.[22] That research, however, didn't include women.

Oops.

Guess what? For women it's a whole different story. An angry female exec is scorned as an out of control, incompetent bitch. Studies have shown that when a man gets angry at work he will be admired, while a woman who displays anger damages her reputation.[23]

## Temper, Temper

*Darren and Colleen were both assigned to the same marketing project under the most critical manager at the company. They both worked long hours, doing painstakingly meticulous edits and were down to their last nerve when their manager, Pat, strolled in with a whole new game plan—effective immediately!*

*Colleen had reached her limit. She loudly complained about all the effort the team had already put in. She insisted that some of the work be salvaged.*

*Pat was unmoved. Ultimately, Colleen pulled herself together and motivated and redirected her crew. A week later, she received a review that included the terms "hysterical" and "inappropriate." Over the next week, her co-manager Darren was subtly made the point man on the deal.*

*Just before the project deadline, Darren was told to make another slew of major revisions. He, like Colleen, finally broke down and expressed his discontent—using profanity for emphasis.*

*But in Darren's case, Pat took him aside and actually apologized for the last minute changes. Pat even consoled Darren, "I know how frustrating it must be!"*

*Colleen was eventually managed out to a different department. Darren was promoted to VP.*

Victoria Brescol, a post-doctoral scholar at Yale, headed a study titled, "When Can Angry Women Get Ahead?"[24] The answer appears to be: not very often. In the study, both men and women disapproved of angry women workers and assigned them lower salaries.

"It's an attitude that's not conscious," the study's author wrote. "People are hardly aware of it. [This creates a] difficult paradox" for professional women. Now, that's an understatement. Although biologically women have a greater tendency to express feelings, workplace culture penalizes women who emote, yet rewards men who act out. It's a difficult paradox indeed.

Repressed emotions have been shown to cause stress that can lead to all sorts of ailments, including high blood pressure, diabetes, obesity, heart disease, depression—even chronic eczema! Who needs it? Many women throw in the towel, others simply burn out.

### GOLD-DIGGING GIRL FACT

25% of female Harvard MBAs who graduated in the 1970s had left work completely by the 1990s

*Ann Crittenden, The Price of Motherhood*

Ask a businessman what's wrong with his female co-workers and his initial reticence will give way to a barrage of complaints detailing the deficiencies of working women. Ann Crittenden writes that the beef could be summarized by this simple sentence, "Women aren't men."

One exec broke it down for the researchers. "What's important is my comfort level with a co-worker. It's about collaborations, relationships, and chemistry." Top male execs say that a woman's problem is that she isn't tough enough, she doesn't play golf and, perhaps most offensive of all, she doesn't enjoy sport fishing.

Other studies support these observations on a biological level. Work environments favor women who have high testosterone. (Yes, you mean lady bosses who make all our lives miserable, we're talking to you.) Career women have higher levels of testosterone than non-working women, according to sexologist Theresa Crenshaw. Look, we've all heard of roid rage, caused by steroids that are the big daddy to our old friend testosterone. It's a known fact that testosterone makes people more aggressive, more competitive, and sometimes downright mean.

**GOLD-DIGGING GIRL QUOTE:**

I'm tough, I'm ambitious and I know exactly what
I want. If that makes me a bitch, okay.

*Madonna*

Biologically, men have the testosterone advantage and we all know they don't always play nice. Incivility in the workplace is on the rise and most of it is coming from men. This is backed up by research from the Yale School of Management that says men account for 70% of all rude behavior at work.[25] And in a corollary observation, male managers were found to be seven times more likely to be nasty toward their subordinates than their female counterparts.[26]

In her book *The Feminine Mistake*, Leslie Bennetts notes that many women cannot thrive in the current cultural landscape of the work world. "Women aren't prepared for the ugly mindset at these places . . . the lack of civility factor is huge," one working gal told Bennetts. "Those places treat people like shit."[27]

So after all our attempts to play by the rules of Boy's Nation, it's sad that so many of us find we're back where we were in the pre-feminist era—with limited voice or choice. Economic models can precisely calculate the value of having choices. This is known as "option value." Many (mostly men) have profited from options and option value on Wall Street, while most of us ladies idle away our personal option value. We let the clock run out while we struggle to get ahead in the workplace only to find that there is no "ahead." There's only banging our heads against the Plexiglass.

## BOTTOM LINE

Don't get mad, get married.

## CHAPTER 13

# Frustration: Sex and the Successful Woman

*Men are taught to apologize for their weaknesses, women for their strengths.*

LOIS WYSE, AUTHOR

As mentioned, there *are* successful women in the work-place—just not in great numbers or at the highest levels as once envisioned. And as we rise to the mid-range of the workplace hierarchy, we find an annoying byproduct of our success:

*As women advance in the workplace, the pool of eligible romantic partners is drastically reduced.*

Bummer.

As a woman moves up the ladder, she probably doesn't realize that she's undermining her chances for serious sexual liaisons. Maureen Dowd observed in her book, *Are Men Necessary?*, that "it took women a few decades to realize that everything they were doing to advance themselves in the boardroom [was] sabotaging their chances in the bedroom."[28]

Power in a woman can be an aphrodisiac—but a smart, funny, successful woman can also be genuinely intimidating. Patty Stangler, who runs a matchmaking service for millionaire men in Los Angeles and is the host of her own reality show, puts it in even more straightforward terms: "When you lead with your career, their ding dong dangler just neutralizes and goes down."

Remember Sharon and Ted? After heavy duty flirtation at the office, they were enjoying their first date . . .

*As they selected dessert from the tasting menu, Ted was busy trying to cop a better look at Sharon's nipple and she was trying to think of other ways to impress him. She casually mentioned her recent raise and reached for her wallet to pick up the tab. Ted did a quick calculation and realized Sharon was bringing in almost twice his salary. Without really knowing why, his mind began to drift to naughty thoughts about the pretty young woman who had recently been hired as his assistant.*

Let's face it, who doesn't know a hardworking girlfriend or wife who got dumped for a secretary, hostess, nanny or some other service femme? For many men, once they are successful, they don't want parity, they want to party. Several studies have shown that these men don't like to compete with the women they're sleeping with—they want to dominate them (which some of us may actually like, but that's a different book).

> **GOLD-DIGGING GIRL QUOTE**
>
> Men do not want to date low-earning women, but once a woman starts earning too much they seem to be scared off.
>
> *Steven D. Levitt and Stephen J. Dubner, Freakonomics*

To the self-actualized woman who can both bring home and cook the bacon, this may be the kind of news that makes one's blood boil. Theresa Crenshaw writes, "When a modern woman reaches for the check, she doesn't realize that she is interfering with an ancient biological imperative . . . If you want to sabotage a relationship . . . pull out your American Express card." The modern career girl might exclaim, "This doesn't make sense! Why shouldn't we be able to treat our date to dinner?"

But this gets right to the heart of the GDI. In many ways, we humans are still primitive. No matter how equal a couple's finances, most men still want to feel like they're providing. They want to feel superior and anything else is emasculating.

In some circles, if a woman makes more money than her spouse or boyfriend, she will often pretend in public that she doesn't so he can look and feel more masculine. But no matter how carefully hidden, sometimes this power imbalance can be the death of a relationship.

## A New York Story

*Gloria and Nigel were a power couple in New York City. She worked as a producer at a major TV network and he owned a trendy gallery in SoHo. Then Nigel's gallery fell out of favor and his business floundered. Nigel rallied to organize a do-or-die art show featuring mostly his own edgy and provocative paintings.*

*The show bombed.*

*Meanwhile, Gloria was promoted. She was suddenly the rising star of the newsroom. While her career soared and his soured, Nigel lost interest in Gloria sexually. She too found him less and less attractive.*

*Instead, Gloria became more and more interested in her highly paid, highly creative co-worker, an Emmy-Award-winning editor who sported some sweet tattoos and a ponytail that some might think was a little too long—not her. One night, crashing a story together in the wee hours of the morning, she found herself bent over the Avid Editing System with her Perlas down around her knees and Ponytail mounting her from behind.*

*Though the affair with Ponytail eventually fizzled, it was a turning point for Gloria. She felt powerful and sexy. She began to resent having to pay for Nigel's acrylics, canvases and steadily rising pay-per-view monthly bill. Meanwhile, her success continued to emasculate Nigel. They tried to keep it together, but in the end a 10-year relationship ended in divorce.*

*He told her when he left that he was "tired of people viewing him as the woman of the house." He took up with a model from his life-drawing class who makes minimum wage and thinks he's an amazing (if struggling) artist.*

*Gloria, a stylish and successful woman, was recently named co-executive producer of a hit show and hasn't been approached for a date in years.*

Doesn't it seem like every time a girl is successful in the workplace men believe it's a *de facto* commentary on their masculinity? They're mad at us when we beat them at their own games. Why do you think the word "biatch"❤ has become so ubiquitous in our common parlance?

Of course there are exceptions to the rule of "men-on-top," examples of what we like to call "reverse couples." She's the hard driving investment banker and he's the good-looking

---

❤ Gangster Rap term for *bitch*, which, according to UrbanDictionary.com, "somehow has found its way into the mouths of every white teen in America." Alternate spelling: beotch.

underachiever. Remember Demi Moore's movie *Disclosure* in which the gorgeous high-powered female exec forced her underlings into compromising positions? Remember Demi Moore marrying sit-com lightweight Ashton Kutcher? See, it does happen, but apparently only to Demi Moore.

Just like fabulously beautiful models who can't find a date, successful and powerful women find limited options when it comes to men. First off, an ordinary guy just isn't going to feel comfortable nuzzling up to say ... a Condi Rice. Let's face it, the pool of viable suitors tends to dry up as you climb the ladder.

Dating down isn't really an option for most successful gals. While a man can still get a boost from consorting with a sexy young gal who doesn't earn, a woman doesn't get a professional, social or financial boost from dating a hot young guy with empty pockets. For that to be worthwhile he better be damn good in bed—and, sadly that doesn't count for squat in the long run.

### BOTTOM LINE

Empowering ourselves economically can undermine our sexual power. Maybe that's why smart girls marry money.

## CHAPTER 14

# Flex-Time:
# The Working Mother

*Any woman who can't afford a nanny
shouldn't have children.*

CORPORATE SUPERVISOR, TO A NEW MOM

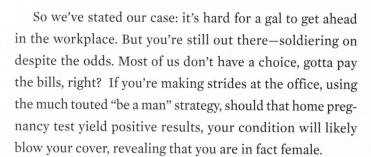

So we've stated our case: it's hard for a gal to get ahead in the workplace. But you're still out there—soldiering on despite the odds. Most of us don't have a choice, gotta pay the bills, right? If you're making strides at the office, using the much touted "be a man" strategy, should that home pregnancy test yield positive results, your condition will likely blow your cover, revealing that you are in fact female.

Once you stop vomiting into your plastic desk-side garbage can and your bump starts to show, your non-mommy cohorts may secretly grumble, knowing the extra burden your pregnancy is likely to put on them. Meanwhile, your very presence at the office is immediately altered: your body grows daily, causing you to lumber slowly about the workplace on your frequent trips to the ladies room.

Internally your body is marinating in extremely high doses of pregnancy hormones that are changing you in even more profound ways. As noted in Dr. Louann Brizendine's bestseller *The Female Brain*, a pregnant woman's "brain is altered—structurally, functionally and in many ways, irreversibly."

It will be no surprise to many to learn that during the last trimester, studies show pregnant women's brains actually *shrink*. That may be why they can't find their keys. On the other hand, Brizendine notes that the cortex, the thinking center of the brain, actually grows larger—perhaps preparing for the rigors of mommyhood. The good news is our brains are flexible and go back to normal a few months after birth. But by that time you also have a newborn to deal with, so having your old brain back may not really help that much, considering the resulting sleep deprivation and your new fave perfume: *Eau du Baby Vomit*.

**GOLD-DIGGING GIRL FACT**

Among corporate executives who earn $100,000 a year or more, 49% of the women did not have children, compared with only 10% of men.

*Maureen Dowd, Are Men Necessary?*

Once junior comes along, you'll quickly find that you have two demanding jobs. Because no matter how egalitarian your romantic partnership, it turns out that traditional gender roles tend to take over after baby. How can they not? Having bathed in pregnancy hormones for months, from the first minute Mommy holds and smells the scent of her newborn, she can experience a crazy rush many new mothers describe as falling deeply in love. Now there's science to back it up; those new brain scans show that once a woman has bonded with her newborn, her romantic love center is all lit up again.

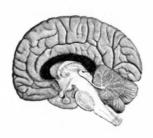

It's not the same for Dad. His hormonal make-up has not changed as radically. No matter how much fathers love their little ones and are elated by the birth of their children, let's get real—men can't actually provide food through their nipples.

It's not just breastfeeding—motherhood is more than a full-time job. One study estimated that it would take 17 different professions to replace the work of one full-time mom. A few among these might include chauffeur, play-date coordinator, tutor, therapist, on-demand chef, snot-nose and ass wiper, stylist, coach, maid, Lego-important-missing-piece finder, nurse, banker, arbitrator, judge, jury and executioner. It's a hell of a gig for a go-getter but the pay scale often sucks.

So it's back to work we go. When you return from your much-resented maternity leave—whether it was three weeks or seven months—you'll realize the term "balancing act" is far too euphemistic to describe what you're attempting to do. It's more like performing pirouettes with a buzzing Blackberry in one hand and a breast pump in the other. With motherhood, women are practically forced to become instant superheroes. We invest ourselves fully in two important and disparate missions: achieving at work, while raising and nurturing our children (three missions if you count trying to maintain a relationship with the baby-Daddy). Our "Clark Kent" side heads off to the office, never knowing when Super-Mom will have to emerge. She's always just a phone call away.

## SuperMom

*Nurse practitioner and midwife Mariana has a son, Alberto, who attends a pricey preschool that has a policy of "checking in" with parents when a student is troubled. But during the workday, it sometimes feels more like harassment. When she sees the school's caller ID on her cell as she's walking in to perform a pelvic exam, Mariana immediately knows it's time to switch gears.*

*SuperMom dashes into an empty exam room, flips open her cell phone and imagines herself in a form-fitting superhero get-up. She checks her watch and assures her son that she'll be home for dinner. Although it was an interruption in her overscheduled day, she's glad that at least this time she didn't have to leave to pick him up.*

*Despite working full-time, Mariana gets to participate in her son's schooling. But she often feels stretched on the rack of working motherhood, pulled in opposing directions. For the moment, the current crisis is solved, and she switches back to professional mode, with her white coat and her vaginal speculum. She's off, another mission to accomplish.*

Despite what some popular TV shows might claim, it's hard to be a superhero. But millions of us do it every day—in fact, 75% of moms with kids under 18 work and 50% of them work full-time.[29] But at the end of the day, we sometimes find we can't keep up. We forget to stock the fridge and when forced to dash out for a gallon of milk, we can't help but throw in something for stress relief—a gossip rag or a pack of smokes. Perhaps even a tiny bottle of high-quality tequila and a lime.

On top of that, lots of families can't find good daycare or affordable nannies that can stand in for us. The latest studies tell us that the children of full-time working moms *can* be well-nurtured by a babysitter as long as the sitter is loving and truly attentive to a child's needs. They just aren't that easy to find. Too bad there's no "Mary Poppins" category on Craigslist.

## Mission Impossible?

*After her divorce, Star didn't know it would be so challenging to find decent childcare for her two young daughters. A friend referred Nanny #1, who charmed Star immediately. She hired her on the spot. But days later, Star unexpectedly came home for lunch to find the nanny's well-tattooed and well-hung boyfriend standing naked in the kitchen eating a vegan meal he had just prepared.*

*She paid a higher hourly rate for Nanny #2, whose letters of recommendation were truly impressive. Unfortunately, Star had to fire her, after her youngest daughter announced how pretty the nanny looked wearing Mommy's best jewelry and favorite outfit from Neiman's.*

*Finally Star called a highly rated agency and interviewed a woman she thought was the perfect candidate. But Star couldn't*

*pull the trigger when she learned the agency fee was close to*
*$5,000. For now, Star has her girls in daycare. But she's noticed*
*a change in them: They seem more angry and aggressive.*

Star is worried and guilt-ridden. Like many working
moms, she's still searching for the perfect solution.

Some mothers are forced by economic circumstances to
leave their children in what could be dangerous circumstances every day. The daycare option is a mixed bag. Onsite
daycare seems like the ideal solution: A busy working mom
can still check in on her child throughout the day. Unfortunately, it's become a reality in only a few places, and for many
the waiting lists are so long that junior won't get accepted
until shortly after his first nocturnal wet dream.

The arguments and research of the pros and cons of daycare itself are always fraught with controversy. A study by the
National Institute of Health[30] followed over 1,300 children
from infancy to sixth grade and found that the longer kids
had spent in daycare before starting kindergarten, the more
likely their sixth-grade teachers were to report problem
behavior, such as getting into fights, acting out, or not following the rules. But many working moms don't have any
other choice.

While comparatively inexpensive, some daycare centers
are beautifully staffed by well-meaning employees, while
others have been known to drug the overactive little ones

with over-the-counter sleep aids to lighten the load.[31] Many moms cannot afford quality daycare at all, but have extended families that help. Others are challenged, like Star, to go through some trial and error in hopes of finding the "village" they need in order to stay in the work force.

If you have money, you may think you're safe—having the ability to hire a full-time professional nanny. But even at the high end, it can be a bit scary. We've all heard of nanny-cam footage and some of us have seen it on the six o'clock news: That nanny who was such a natural with kids is caught dangling the helpless infant upside down or whacking the baby on the head with a wooden spoon.

Over the decades we gals have come up with a few strategies to deal with the complexities of balancing our work and family lives. Many baby boomers chose to establish a career and stash a few bucks in the bank—waiting until nearly eligible to join the AARP before attempting to have kids. But fertility treatments, surrogate motherhood, and legions of 45-year-old mommies pushing strollers with triplets has gotten some younger women asking if maybe there isn't a better way.

In the 1990s, *The New York Times Magazine* announced that a new group of highly educated stay-at-home moms chose not to go back to work after baby. They were called the "Opt Out" generation. The "startling" take-home message of the article was that these women were the fast horses, the good bets, go-getters, Ivy leaguers, lawyers and MBA's. Yet after struggling through all that schoolin', and having had real life experience in top professions, these smart chicks preferred to be at home—far from the workplace—to focus on being good moms.

Lisa Belkin, the author of the now infamous article *The Opt-Out Revolution*,[32] declared that these latte-sipping moms, carrying Dolce & Gabbana diaper bags, decided "they just didn't want to work." The article created tremendous acrimony between many camps for various reasons, not the least of which was the questionable method of the author's research—it seems all she did was call up a few friends she'd made while an undergrad at Princeton and asked what they were up to.

Truth is, plenty of women find out good and quick that the 60-hour work weeks, with all those male bosses and misogynistic expectations, really aren't all that rewarding. One "opt-out" lawyer told us, "Work sucks for the most part, and I didn't want to have to work twice as hard as my male boss to get half as far and miss out on seeing my baby, too."

But Belkin's article had impact, bringing this concept to the masses and highlighting one thing: After marriage and childbirth, many highly competent women feel work is optional. Growing up in a society that promised equality, these women felt their education protected them from hard times. This crowd of super-achiever-about-to-make-partner

moms get married and then drop out believing that their
achievements will allow them easy entrée back into the work
world if necessary.

⏤⏤ ∞ ⏤⏤

Unfortunately, after a few years of full-time at-home
mothering, many women have found few on-ramps back into
the work force. In her book, *The Feminine Mistake*, Leslie
Bennetts wags her finger at young women—warning that it's
a grave error to leave work. She makes a good point. Your
resume does start to look yellowed with age as your college
graduation date fades into the distant past and there's that
five-year gap since you last worked. You look like damaged
goods in the competitive hiring marketplace.

Bennetts suggests that women "just suck it up" for what
she calls the "fifteen year paradigm," when you'll just have to
balance work and parenthood. Too bad if it's hard for you,
your family, or your kids. She sees no other way.

It can be done, she assures her readers, after all, she did it
herself.

But her argument is flawed. Ms. Bennetts, once a *New
York Times* journalist who gets bragging rights for being one
of the first reporters to interview Hillary Clinton, has a job
that lends itself to flexibility. In her book, she describes typing
away on her laptop while waiting for her kids in the carpool

lane at school. She espouses being more like her, finding other ways to be flexible with your work since your work won't be flexible for you.

We took exception to this suggestion, noting that a few jobs can't be performed while waiting outside your kid's school. Among them are transplant surgeon, secretary, accountant, cashier, toll-booth operator, and call girl, unless you have a van. We could go on, but you probably get the point. Bennetts also mentions in her book that "like me, most of my close friends have stable marriages, wonderful children and satisfying careers." We were left pondering only one thing, "Are there Stepford Wives in your neighborhood, too?"

Once upon a time, social commentators imagined a utopian future where working mothers would benefit from a vibrant part-time or job-sharing work culture, but it hasn't come to pass. Instead we have a cut-throat, spike-heeled culture that makes us feel guilty about having a family. Many bosses think that women who work part-time have a recreational attitude toward their jobs and bosses don't keep these gals in mind for promotion or a raise, even if they just made the cover of *Parenting Magazine* as Mother of the Year.

We've been around long enough to know that most ambitious go-getters tend to think rules don't apply to them. They'll ignore Bennetts' advice. They'll stay at home with baby and plan to find an equal or better job when and if they go back to work at all.

Forget it, girls, that position has been filled. Oh, and yeah, one more thing, remember that kid you used to babysit? Well, she's just graduated from college with thousands of other energetic fire-starters eager to take your old job.

Along with their youth, most of these new grads are unencumbered by children. Bennetts also quotes a stat you may not have heard: A study by a Cornell University sociologist says mothers are 44% less likely to be hired than non-mothers who have the same resume, qualifications and experience.[33] So yes, Ms. Bennetts does have a point. It's a puzzle to ponder for the smart girl turned breeder.

Why would an employer care if you have kids? Because if your child is under six you will have twice the rate of absenteeism compared to co-workers.[34] Because if there's a sudden need for overtime you can't stay if you have kids to feed or pick up or chauffeur. Of course there's a law—or there ought to be—preventing this kind of discrimination. But when employers justify their actions on the basis of "not the right fit," they can get away with virtually anything. And they do. So in addition to ageism and sexism, we also have to deal with "mommyism."

On the upside, more moms are slowly breaking into some higher ranking jobs (if not the *tip top* echelons). We have heard a few stories of moms-who-are-also bosses who not only respect motherhood, but also see the multitasking attributes of the SuperMom as a workplace asset. One executive producer recently gave our friend Ellen a promotion saying, "You're a mom, you can easily manage these people." As we've mentioned, progress is slow, but this is a promising development.

On the other hand, in many cases the workplace is downright hostile to motherhood. The women who really get ahead know this and have raised the bar for the rest of us.

## Bringing Up Baby

*Vanessa, an Ivy League MBA and female partner at a high-end consulting firm, startled her male colleagues by showing up pregnant for the first time at the age of 38. But she weathered the pregnancy with ease, as though she was simply wearing a basketball strapped to her belly. She never missed a last minute overseas trip, a meeting, or an all-night brain-storming session.*

*Everyone wondered how she would handle her pregnancy leave. She never discussed the matter with her team. Then on cue at 40 weeks, she gave vaginal birth on a Saturday (saving the cord blood) and sailed into the office at 7 a.m. on Monday morning lugging her newborn in a car seat. She set the contraption down in the corner, plugged a binky into baby Madison's mouth, and ran her team meeting while teleconferencing in the Tokyo and London offices.*

*Within the week, baby Madison's highly paid au pair arrived from Europe and Vanessa became a living legend at the firm.*

Since only 10% of the partners at this particular firm are women, indeed Vanessa might have had super-powers to get to her exalted position, including a magical snatch that healed on command. But for the rest of us without yogic yonis and $500,000 a year salaries, mixing work and care for a newborn puts stresses on the workplace.

If you're not super-rich and can't afford a nanny, in the view of many employers, daring to have kids is practically a crime. So the less encumbered by family, the better. Indeed noted author Linda Hirshman suggests that we should look to mainland China for our childbearing strategies and offered up her opinion that all women should work *and* have no more than one child.

∽∾∽

On the other hand, most men who really make it have at-home wives picking up the slack and the kids from school. Two out of three male executives and 80% of CFOs have stay-at-home wives. A study from the *Harvard Business Review* basically concluded that, due to our biology, women are more expensive to hire than men.

Then there's the problem of what happens to a working mom who opts out and then gets divorced. Be forewarned. If your husband decides to leave you, the judge in your divorce court is likely to agree with the younger you. He'll assume that you can breeze back into the work place and pick up where you left off. When he decides the amount of your alimony, he will likely impute your income to what you might have been making if you hadn't indulged in the "luxury" of staying at home instead of returning to work.

## Daddy Daycare

Now even as we whine and moan and bitch about how tough it is out there for working moms, there's a new type of dad emerging that suggests a promising trend. Just as it is for women holding the title of CEO, the sightings of this animal known as the "SuperDad" are rare, but increasing. Truth be told, raising kids is hard and moms just can't do it all alone.

There's definitely a cultural shift—it's hip to be Dad. Or maybe there's a genetic drift causing more sensitive genes to be expressed in males. We don't know, but when our parents were raising kids, Dad really didn't do much to help. These days, seeing Dad pushing a stroller or even wrangling his twin six-year-olds at Legoland doesn't make onlookers point and stare.

Many modern dads actually know how to mix formula, apply sunscreen, make lunches, and pack all the necessities *without being nagged by their wives*. Even rich and famous guys like Brad Pitt are getting into it. We think this is a good omen, although the statistics still say that only 1% of children have a man as a full-time caregiver, and many of those daddies have a girlfriend, sister or good-old mom standing in for them, according to Andrew Cherlin, a Professor of Sociology at Johns Hopkins University.

Even if your Baby-Daddy doesn't help with dirty diapers, he still has an important role to play. When the ladies who graduated from Harvard in the 1970s were interviewed in the 1990s, the ones who'd managed to "have it all" were the ones that had supportive mates. Those who floundered in their careers after having a family suggested that "the kind of man they had married had fatally sabotaged their plans."

### BOTTOM LINE

The data suggest that when trying to find our way in the world, the most important decision we can make is our choice of mate. And by now, you know what we're talking about.

## CHAPTER 15

# Fads & Fashion: A Timeline

**_Never think you've seen the last of anything._**

EUDORA WELTY, AUTHOR

As we've seen, we gals, working women, stay-at-home moms, FemiNasties, and regular smart girls have lots of differences and lots of things in common. But what makes us tick? Often, we ourselves aren't really sure.

*"What do women want?"* Sigmund Freud famously pondered this question as if it were a koan: something "inaccessible to rational understanding."

Of course, it was meant to be a put-down, to cast women in the role of inscrutable chimera—part man, part breast. For most of history, women have been at center-stage of men's wonderment, attention, and sexual fantasies. We put forth

our best efforts to get their attention, beget them fine children, and keep a perfectly tidy home. They held us up and
held us down at the same time. And sometimes, we even
liked it.

Now they're not sure what do to with us.

In part this is because we haven't known what to do with
ourselves—*we* have been stooges of Freud, suckers for fads,
and slaves to the fashions of the day. But for the sake of
making sure everyone is on the same page, let's review a
recent timeline.

**1800s–1940s:** Susan B. Anthony leads her Suffragettes
in a fight to win American women the right to vote. It takes
decades for men to give it up and even then it's given
begrudgingly. Most women aspire only to be good wives and
raise families. For the upper classes, females are practically
invisible in the male-dominated workplace, unless there's a
war on. This time marks the beginning of the end for
arranged marriages in the Western world. Thanks to a con-
vergence of ideas of the Enlightenment and economic
trends, the new ideal marriage morphs from one based on
political and economic alliances to marriage based on love.
At the turn of the century, Sigmund Freud introduces the
concept of penis envy, which ultimately influences the way

society views women, relegating us to sexual second-class citizens.

*Actress Jane Russell in a publicity shot for Howard Hughes' film* The Outlaw

Flat-chested flappers are the hot trend of the 20s, but by the 40s Jane Russell and her giant breasts become huge stars in the film *The Outlaw*, thanks to a specially designed underwire push-up bra invented by aerospace engineer and Hollywood tycoon Howard Hughes. The release of the *The Outlaw* was delayed for three years due to cries about Russell's indecency, but in the end, the boobs carried the day. No one has any idea what is happening for women below the waist because (show some common decency!) it just isn't discussed.

*Marilyn Monroe, c. 1953*

**The 50s:** Marilyn Monroe is the ultimate pin-up girl who stars in a comedic movie called *How to Marry a Millionaire.* Girls are taught that creating the ideal home and family life—including a freshly made cocktail and slippers to hand to a successful husband when he returns home from work—is the ultimate goal. Should that fail, they have a possible back-up plan as a secretary, teacher or nurse. Hugh Hefner launches *Playboy* magazine, which for the first time in American history tells men that being a responsible husband really isn't *all that.* The magazine's first feature article, "Miss Gold-Digger 1953," declares that "a couple of generations ago, this was a man's world and a nice young woman had a difficult time making her own way. Nothing could be further from the truth in 1953. Even the simplest wench can make a handsome living today." Rock and roll emerges: Elvis and hula hoops—it's all about the swinging hips, baby. Women want hourglass figures—big boobs are highly fashionable. Women still have pubic hair, but in the girly mags, the bush is airbrushed or the model discreetly positions her actual "private parts" out of view.

*Audrey Hepburn as "Holly Golightly" in Breakfast at Tiffany's.*

**The 60s:** Audrey Hepburn becomes a film icon in *Breakfast at Tiffany's*, by playing a New York City girl who gets by on the good graces of her wealthy boyfriends. Betty Friedan, author and feminist activist, publishes *The Feminine Mystique* in 1963, voicing the dissatisfaction felt by women whose *only* role came from caring for husbands and children. She asserts that the idyllic homes of the 1950's are more like prison than paradise and launches a contemporary feminist movement. The first birth control pill hits the market giving women more sexual freedom than ever before. At the same time, the Civil Rights movement dominates the decade and real progress is made for African Americans. The Beatles come to America, giving us Beatlemania. Breasts are set free. Hippie girlfriends take acid and offer free love, but *still* have to cook dinner for their radical male boyfriends. The bush is *au naturel*.

*Farrah Fawcett, angel of the '70s*

**The 70s:** Farrah Fawcett is star of the TV show *Charlie's Angels*. Gloria Steinem publishes *Ms. Magazine*, while NOW—the National Organization for Women—becomes politically powerful. NOW founder Betty Friedan is cast out, but the feminist movement has a major impact. Bored couples in the suburbs swap sex partners in "key parties." Twenty million mood rings are sold. In the pick up scene, savvy men wearing wide-collar polyester shirts replace the old pick up line, "What's your sign?" with "I love you for your mind." Radical politics gives way to even more popular use of recreational drugs. The Beatles take acid and break up. Breasts are still swinging free for "women's libbers," but for the rest of us, they're securely encased back in the bra. Pubic hairstyles are still natural. Some men even like a really "big bush."

*Madonna, the "Material Girl" c. 1983; Pamela Anderson, "CJ", c. 1989*

**The 80s:** Madonna's song "Material Girl" turns her into an instant icon, but we girls still don't get the message. Instead of becoming gold-diggers we become sluts, chasing after boy toys. Consumerism is king. Greed is good. Friedan is forgotten. Women head to work in power suits with shoulder pads and everybody becomes a "yuppie." The woman's dream of "having it all" is born. Cyndi Lauper's "Girls Just Want to Have Fun" dominates pop radio. Ronald Reagan is everybody's daddy. AIDS & condoms: Sex=Fear. Conservative trends trump the radical notions of the preceding decades. By the end of the 1980s, the ideal boobs are gravity-defying balloons as defined by Baywatch's CJ, played by Pamela Anderson, romping bra-less through the surf in yet another red bathing suit. The "bikini line" is in vogue, with the hair "down there" worn as a neatly trimmed triangle. Pubic deforestation has begun.

*Female icons of the 1990s ranged from playful to powerful.*

**The 90s:** Spice Girls. Buff Linda Hamilton in *Terminator II*. Girl Power. Tweens. Nine-year-old girls on diets. The rise of term "Feminazi" has women running scared. Even female PhD students proudly declare that they are "not feminists"—but of course they still want equal pay, demonstrating that even the smartest girls are completely confused. Naomi Wolf declares in her book *The Beauty Myth* that feminism is the new "F-word." Madonna makes headlines with her S & M coffee table book: *Sex*. OJ brings domestic violence out of the shadows. Monica Lewinsky brings down the President. Fake boobs begin to dominate the landscape, even for teens. For regular women, the bush is still trimmed at bikini line. Penthouse Pets and strippers style their pubic hair in a shape vaguely reminiscent of Hitler's mustache.

*Brit and Madge making out on stage, MTV Video Music Awards, 2003.*

**The 00s:** Madonna again, now tonguing a young blonde *superstar* on stage, while penning children's books and adopting a child from a small African nation. *Sex and the City* defines womanhood for single gals and *Girls Gone Wild* defines coming-of-age for teens. A top-rated network TV show features a bored housewife in expensive high heels screwing her underage gardener. Suburban moms do exercise routines on stripper poles. The rise of the celebrity nitwits: Jessica Simpson and Paris Hilton. Shows like *Real Sex* and *Cat House* bring semi-soft porn into the mainstream. Vaginal rejuvenation is the new boob job, proving that even our most intimate parts need to be retrofitted to meet the evermore rigid beauty standards. Botox is now *de rigueur*. The "Brazilian" is practically a household word: the bush has been shaved, waxed, lasered and/or tweezed in favor of pre-pubescent baldness or a tiny "landing strip."❤

Along with the loss of our pubic hair, have we also lost our credibility? Just look at the condensed history above. As a group we femmes don't seem to be making any sense at all. In fact, what *do* we want? Men have obviously picked up on our confusion and, perhaps justifiably, simply want us to shut up and take our clothes off.

No matter how accomplished women become, the primitive preoccupation with scoring a mate dominates the timeline. We'll always employ the latest technology—from hydraulic bras to surgical enhancement of our birth canals—to make ourselves more sexually desirable.

Yet as we've previously noted, when women make gains in the man's world, we often lose our sexual power. This might explain the somewhat baffling trend of total deforestation of our nether regions. Why is it fashionable for com-

---

❤ Side note, Men (or women) who enjoy porn and want to see pubic hair are now sent to the "fetish" aisle, or can pick up a "classic" from the used section.

petent *women* to mimic 10-year-old girls underneath their power suits?

## BOTTOM LINE

As we've become more liberated and powerful, sex as currency hasn't gone away—it's become mainstream. It seems for every two economic steps forward we take, we also stop to give a lap dance.

CHAPTER 16

# Fugly or Femilicious?

*I'm so beautiful, sometimes people
weep when they see me.*

MARGARET CHO, COMEDIAN

～⸎～

So here we are waxing and shaving in a vain attempt to stay forever 21. And why not? Women in their twenties are sexual magnets *regardless of their looks*, according to sexologist Theresa Crenshaw. Even if you don't believe it, all girls are beautiful when young. In our reproductive peak, we are juicy and oozing sexual messages irresistible to the male species.[35] Unfortunately, most of us don't know this until we're in our forties and look back longingly at our high school yearbook photos.

If you're still not convinced and deep down you really think that you're a hideous genetic mutant, you're *still* not out of luck. Let's take a step back and consider why you might not believe this. We've all heard the conventional wisdom that beauty is defined by some sort of mathematical symmetry. But some of the most beautiful women in the world don't fit that mold: Uma Thurman, Sarah Jessica Parker, Julia Roberts.

Haven't we all seen tabloid pictures at the check-out stand of celebrities without their makeup? They look just like regular girls—without symmetry and often with, as Richard Burton said about himself, "pores as big as the craters of the moon."

Pretty girls know that the ideal of perfection doesn't hold a candle to grooming, make-up, clothing and attitude. Our friend Amy swears men look at her in a whole new way since her discovery of Botox and an expensive brand of push-up bra. Some of you might even be considering going under the knife. But you may not have to. Here's the story of Jessica and Allison.

## She's Got A Secret

*After Jessica's first child was born she joined a "Mommy and Me" group in San Francisco, California. The mommies demonstrated their one-up-woman-ship by inviting the whole group to their elaborate houses.*

*But when Allison invited the moms, they didn't have high hopes. Allison had described her job before her baby was born as computer geek for a failed internet start-up.*

*The mommies were stunned to find that her house was an expansive multi-level dream home with a pool and a view of the ocean. Her digs threw each of them into a kind of orgasmic state that was only quelled when they answered nature's sudden call to nurse their infants.*

*A "why-her-and-not-me?" kind of envy streamed through their eyes. The savviest of the mommies instantly converted this energy into giggly "best girlfriend" behavior. Comments like "Where did you get that armoire?" and "I love your art!" abounded.*

*Before seeing her house, they barely sniffed in her direction. Why?*

*Because their opinions were contaminated by the media's narrow definition of beauty: They simply thought she was FUGLY!*

*As one of the mommies said, she had the chinless face of a vulture, and a nose to match. Another mommy-dearest described Allison's body as shaped like an exotic bottle of liqueur—wide where it should have been slim, flat where it should have been round. Another, who had once called Allison "unpleasant," suddenly considered that perhaps she was just shy, and gave Allison the number of her dermatologist.*

*Allison informed them off-handedly that her husband was a venture capitalist and former investment banker. Each immediately conjured up an image of the man, one more troll-like than the next.*

*But then her hubby came downstairs and floored them all with the looks of a granite-jawed matinee idol. He leaned over and kissed her. He gazed at her with adoration and longing.*

*He cracked some funny jokes, threw out a few compliments and had the whole group at his feet in a matter of minutes.*

*"What a doll!" they all agreed.*

*"How did she land this prince?" Jessica wondered. "Did she have some sexual secret?"*

Truth is, even if you don't have tantric treasures, you can still find the man of your dreams. *Just being a woman puts you in the game.* Deep down, almost all of us know this. And almost all men, under the right circumstances, will acknowledge universal feminine beauty.

### GOLD-DIGGING GIRL QUOTE

[Life has] endless forms so beautiful and
most wonderful ...

*Charles Darwin, On The Origin of Species*

But we don't have to yearn for something we think we can never become. We have already stated that all of us who are alive today are descendants of life's evolutionary winners. So we all contain the seeds of something irresistibly sexy, even if those seeds haven't yet bloomed.

Harvard Professor Nancy Etcoff, author of *Survival of the Prettiest*, insists that attraction is arbitrary. "It is difficult to put into words why a particular set of eyes or a certain mouth move us while others do not," Etcoff says. "The ideal of beauty exists in the mind, not in the flesh."[36] So one man's *fugly* is another man's *femilicious* (Allison's husband's taste obviously ran to the bird-like).

Still not convinced? Well, if some outside influence has you feeling so flawed that you think that you are downright fugly, take it from us, you've got something that someone will find he can't live without—and that's a bankable fact. Allison's story is proof that even if you aren't a cover girl, you aren't out of the game. In fact, you may even win it.

### GOLD-DIGGING GIRL TIP

If all else fails, you can always go for the short guy. He's funny and sweet and if he earns, he's worth a second look.

# Femininity

We know you're trying. After all, nearly 1,500 tubes of lipstick are sold in this country every minute and we know that they are not all being bought by Gwen Stefani. Playing up our femininity—that quality girls have that guys don't—is the most powerful lure we can dangle. (Men dangle other things.)

But almost every girl we know is waiting to lose that last 10 or 50 pounds before she goes out to hunt her quarry. Who can blame us? Every internet pop-up ad, TV talk show, newscast, magazine cover and radio ad blasts us with the latest ways to improve ourselves: from the Ab Master to the latest must-have skin creams and non-surgical facelifts. The list is endless, and the advertising is powerful.

These images of ideal beauty are digitally enhanced. One of our friends had a full time job air-brushing pimples off Playboy models' asses. So don't buy the lie that you're ugly and unsexy.

Our femininity is an innate part of our architecture, but it's most powerful while we're young. It's then that we are ripe for the picking and our bodies are lusting to copulate and procreate. So girls, we can't afford the luxury of self-pity. We don't have the time to wait for the pounds to drop, or for enough money for a boob job, or for the never-coming approval from Mom. Youth is your power. Use it or lose it.

To our thinking, it seems perfectly natural for a man to want a mate who can maximize his chances of having 1) children and 2) a full and satisfying sex life. Anthropologist David Buss studied more than 10,000 individuals from 37 cultures across five continents.[37] He consistently found that males value physical attractiveness and youth more than women value either looks or wealth.

On the other hand, among chimpanzees, our closest primate relatives, males tend to dig more mature females. "They actively prefer older mothers . . . [They see] the wrinkled skin, ragged ears, bald patches, and elongated nipples . . . as alluring," wrote Boston University researcher Martin Muller in *Current Biology*.[38] He suggests that human males prefer younger women because we have a short breeding window. Chimps stay fertile their whole lives. We know you may not like the term "sell-by date" but those ovaries are like any other carton of eggs—they expire. That's why we gotta use the tiny window of youth for our own personal gain.

In business, an asset (in this case "youth") that declines in value over time is called a "wasting" asset. And while we're still young, enjoying our super-soft skin and resilient muscles, we forget that the clock is ticking. So we girls better get busy while we still have it because our youth and beauty are two of our most powerful assets. But they are wasting assets, losing value by the minute. If you're smart, you can cash them in for a lifetime of financial security. The full-on bimbos do it, so why shouldn't we smart girls do it too?

### GOLD-DIGGING GIRL FACT

Good looks are a woman's most fungible asset, exchangeable for social position, money, and even love.

*Nancy Etcoff, Ph.D, Survival of the Prettiest*

### BOTTOM LINE

You are the offspring of life's evolutionary winners. You are beautiful. Stop feeling sorry for yourself, and go out and work with what you have. Immediately.

CHAPTER 17

# Fuck Yourself

***The good thing about masturbation is that
you don't have to get dressed up for it.***

TRUMAN CAPOTE, WRITER

Okay, so we are out there working with what we've got. Lucky for us, no matter your age, looks or IQ, we all know that women have at least one valuable asset that men don't. It turns out that loving attention to this body part builds confidence and works as a powerful antidote to the love drug.

What do we mean by "loving attention"? We're talking about the "M" word: Masturbation.

Most women don't do it. Formal polls have estimated that just one out of five women plays with herself with any regularity—and only about once a week at that. Informal surveys support this finding. Ask any guy if he jacks off and he'll give you the standard reply, "95% of men say they masturbate and the other 5% are lying." But ask a group of women and their ambivalence shows.

## The Big O

*A few years ago, a group of gals of various ages got together and after a few martinis the discussion turned to sex. Liz had been through two husbands and a total of 25 years of marriage and was embarrassed to admit that she'd never climaxed in all that time. Then, after her second divorce, she had an affair with a hot high school football coach who went down on her for the first time. She experienced her first orgasm, which she called, "The Big O" (Not Oprah).*

*"Wow!" she thought, "now I know what all the fuss is about."*

*Encouraged by her honesty, some of the younger women told their "first time" stories. They were surprised and relieved to find that other women had also struggled to reach orgasm. They discovered that while in college, each started her own personal crusade to figure out why sex was just so . . . unsexy. They read how-to books, got vibrators (or in one case a large, heated cucumber), and created their own curriculum.*

*After many regular afternoon sessions, they taught them-*
*selves to come. This took patience, practice and, in at least one*
*or two instances, trips to the video store to rent porn (this was*
*pre-internet).*

*As for Liz, she wondered why she waited until she was 50,*
*while these girls were experimenting and enjoying their bodies*
*in their teens.*

---

### GOLD-DIGGING GIRL QUOTE

Fifty percent of the women in this country are not
having orgasms. If this were true of the male population,
it would be declared a national emergency.

*Margo St. James, Prostitutes Rights Movement*

---

Remember the breakthrough coffee table women's sexuality bible, *Our Bodies, Ourselves*? Well, it's been updated for
the millennium and you should go buy it. Read it. It may just
inspire you to take a mirror to look closely at what's up down
there.

History proves we can't depend on doctors for the most
up-to-date info on women and their sexuality. In fact, all the
big time medical authorities seem to contradict each other,
from Sigmund Freud to Alfred Kinsey and Masters and

Johnson to the popular self-help gurus Doctors Ruth, Drew and Phil. The work and opinions of all these "sexperts" have affected the way we act and think about sex more than any of us realize.

----- ❦ -----

Freud kicked off the modern era of misinformation by passing judgment about how a woman orgasms. If she needed clitoral stimulation, she was infantile. But a real woman—a mature woman—he pronounced, had vaginal orgasms through intercourse with a man.

In Freud's time, troubled women were viewed as neurotic and had to be cured of their hysteria. Doctors then thought women needed treatment because their "womb fury" made them sick with an array of symptoms, including depression, palpitations, belly pain, cramps, headaches and even ticklishness. [39]

Docs of that era eventually stumbled upon the cure: female pelvic massage. They would manually stimulate their patients until they had orgasms. Sometimes this would take up to an hour and leave the poor physician exhausted. By 1880, doctors' prayers were answered: The first mechanical vibrators became available. Although to the modern man making a woman climax seems like a great work if you can get it, back then it was viewed as, "The job nobody wanted."[40]

"Hanging Type Carpenter Vibrator from Mechanical Vibration and Its
Therapeutic Applications (New York: Scientific Authors, 1904)

All of this information came to light in Rachel Maines' pio-
neering work *The Technology of Orgasm: 'Hysteria,' the Vibrator, and Women's Sexual Satisfaction.* According to Maines, as
word spread, women came in droves to these understanding
healers. The hysterics needed ongoing treatment because
their condition was incurable.

Fifty years later, German physician Ernst Grafenberg iden-
tified a sensitive area inside the vagina that could provoke
orgasms. His medical colleagues ignored his discovery for
years. The sensitive area later became known as the G-Spot.

Around the same time, Dr. Alfred Kinsey published *The
Kinsey Reports* which presented statistics from large numbers
of men and women detailing what they were *really* up to in bed.
Kinsey's work, along with Masters and Johnson's *Human
Sexual Response* (1965), shifted the focus of female pleasure to

the clitoris. And for the next half century, many women believed that clitoral stimulation was the proper way to achieve orgasm.

The next big thing in female sex research came in the 1980s with the rediscovery of the G-Spot. By the 1990s, the little-known publication *On Our Backs* featured a cover article on *female ejaculation*. (What the hell is that?!)

Until recently anatomy textbooks did not show any of this. For centuries the men who drew the female pelvis left the "detailed" diagrams ... blank. But now we know the G-spot is on the vaginal wall next to the female prostate.[41] It's real. You have one. It weighs about 5 grams—about the weight of a nickel. The G-Spot is located about one and a half inches inside the vagina on the front wall—you can locate it easily with your index finger.[42.]

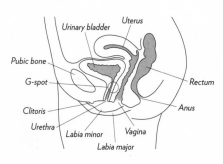

*Female Sexual Anatomy*

Stimulating the G-spot, the clitoris or virtually any part of that area "down there" can lead to orgasm. All these areas are connected by tissue that engorges just like when men get erections. There may be many other "magic buttons" that have yet to be found. So don't wait for the medical community to figure it out. What gives you sexual pleasure is personal and belongs to you and you alone. It's never too late to enjoy discovering yourself. Picking up a book on the subject of female ejaculation worked for our friend Giselle.

## G's Spot

*Giselle was divorced and pushing 40 when she married Russell, a sweet man 15 years her senior. Russell was handsome and had sewn his wild oats pretty much all over the place when he met Giselle and decided to settle down.*

*At first sex was pretty hot, although Russell did tend to get soft (male menopause and all). But with the help of a little blue pill, he put the wood to her and they settled into a comfortable sexual routine. Russell and Giselle weren't setting the bed on fire, but neither one was a sexual dynamo and they were long past expecting fireworks.*

*Then Giselle stumbled across a book by Deborah Sundahl called* Female Ejaculation and The G-Spot.[43] *Giselle had heard of the G-Spot but thought that it was just another myth. She leafed through the book wanting to believe that she too could climax with ease, instead of limiting herself to the intermittent orgasms she had when Russell went down on her.*

*She read, studied and learned. And then she practiced. She found her G-Spot and found how to "wake it up." She had softer, fuller, multiple orgasms, so different than the clitoral kind. One day she actually "ejaculated," which was its own type of mind-blowing experience (read Sundahl's book or see her video for details). When she was comfortable she taught her husband about it.*

*Russell loved Giselle's new sexuality because he could stimulate her without having to get it up. On their second night doing G-spot massage, she came four times with his hand inside her. He was so excited by this that he became as hard as a 20-year-old. He entered her and they came together for the first time in their married life.*

After being sexually active for twenty years, Giselle still needed a manual and a really patient partner in order to fully enjoy her orgasms. For us women, prone to introspection and brain chatter, it's often hard for us to drop our cares and focus on sensory pleasures. According to researcher Elizabeth A. Lloyd, women reliably experience orgasm during intercourse about 20% of the time, whereas for men it's more like 100%.[44]

Louann Brizendine, in *The Female Brain*, says that women appear to have a reaction during sex wherein our brains begin chattering. Instead of slowing down and focusing on our physical pleasure, many of us cannot turn off that thinking brain.

It's like the old joke:

**Q:** *"What are most women thinking during sex?"*
**A:** *"Beige. I think I'll paint the ceiling beige."*

What we're thinking about when we hop into bed has a lot to do with cultural expectations. Often women are embarrassed about their bodies or they worry if they are "doing it right." In *The G-Spot: And Other Discoveries about Human Sexuality*, the authors open the book by pointing out that we're never separate from our cultural context. We're always worried if we're doing it right.

If a woman is fearful, anxious or guilty, the pleasure circuits from the genitals to the brain shut down, according to Dr. Louann Brizendine, who studies female sexuality. Brain scans back up her findings: For a woman to orgasm her worry center must be deactivated. And there's one more unexpected finding—her feet must be warm.

### GOLD-DIGGING GIRL TIP

Instead of lingerie, ask for socks.

In addition to warm, fuzzy socks, another important way to help cross the finish line to orgasm is, unfortunately, working out. But the good news is that this kind of work out you can do in your car at a stop light and you hardly have to break a sweat. We're talking about working out your pelvic muscles like you're stopping a stream of urine. Forget about six-pack abs, you're looking for a pumped pelvis. Some of these exercises are known as Kegels and you can Google them and choose your favorite.

If you've never had an orgasm, be patient. You may still consider masturbation a taboo. Many women still feel shame when it comes to the M-word. Feeling guilty about masturbating is ubiquitous; there's even a Catholic saying in Rome that goes, "If you masturbate, the angels will cry." In the original Italian they say, "Se ti tocchi, gli angiolletti piangono." Pretty, isn't it? It almost makes you want to touch yourself.

We're no angels, but it brings tears to our eyes that so many women aren't exploring or enjoying their sexuality. Since we want what's best for you, you should know that masturbation and orgasms improve your health. Climaxing decreases pain, increases your sense of well-being, decreases illness, and can be downright delicious.

## BOTTOM LINE

Fuck yourself. Learn your body. Do whatever it takes. (May we suggest the Hitachi Wonder Wand with the G-Spot attachment?) And by all means, have fun!

## GOLD-DIGGING GIRL SIDEBAR

Still can't find your G-Spot? Not sure if it's a myth? Well, if you're willing to get to know your own body, you can prove to yourself once and for all that the G-Spot is real. All you have to do is give yourself the finger! We mean this literally. This is a masturbation technique, so stop reading if this isn't your thing.

Stick your middle finger into your vagina as far as you can. Bend it slightly like you are beckoning a lover, in a "come hither" shape. Now slide it left and right slowly. Left, right. Left, right. You will notice that there is a soft tube of tissue and on each side it has ridges. Take a deep breath and push down from your belly like you are forcing out the last of a pee that's taking forever to come out. You will notice the area you are massaging will get larger and this will help you locate your G-spot. Keep sliding your finger left and right and then slowly begin to pull it out.

If you can relax your body and concentrate on your vajay-jay, you'll find an area that's MORE sensitive. In the middle, well, right there, it's the hump of your vaginal wall. See the difference? Go back to the spot that was sensitive. You've found it. Don't worry if there are no fireworks (that's stuff for the movies, anyway). That spot holds a lot of your secrets.

Deborah Sundahl, who might be called the G-spot guru, is calling all women to explore this region in order to experience a whole different way to orgasm. She is a pioneer for "G-spot massage," and she reports that this simple technique has been shown to increase the sensitivity of the vagina for many women who could not reach orgasm at all, women who could not come through intercourse, women who only climaxed through cunnilingus, and women who thought they were coming but were just faking it all these years. Reach down and touch yourself.

Wake up your G-Spot. It's yours to enjoy [45].

## CHAPTER 18

# Foraging:
# Gold-Digging in Action

*I'm so sick of everyone saying I*
*married my husband for his money. It just so*
*happens I get turned on by liver spots.*

ANNA NICOLE SMITH

———◦◦◦———

So here we sit satisfied and confident, and now we are ready to begin our quest for financial security. By studying others who've had success navigating this terrain, a beginning gold-digger can gain know-how from those who successfully blazed the trail.

## TFC

*Natasha was not a beauty, but she knew how to work with what she had. She had never been academically inclined, but* she was smart enough to know that she didn't want to live her mother's life: widowed at 34 with three young children. Natasha's mom took two jobs, one of which involved cleaning toilets. Natasha didn't want any part of that.

When she turned 18, she began looking for a way out—her own personal sugar daddy. She found him and, best of all, she felt she might actually be in love. Tall and handsome, he was a podiatrist, specializing in the foot ailments of the New York elite. They married and soon after she bore him three children. Not long after that she found herself in a quandary that many wives encounter—she was getting bored. On the one hand, she admired her husband for his pro-bono trips abroad to surgically correct the malformed feet of Asian children. On the other hand, she was left out, home alone caring for the kids.

Over time she came to feel isolated and lonely. Then one day she freaked out when she found his stash of Asian porn hidden under a loose floorboard. It began to look like his frequent charitable overseas travel involved more than the salvation of disabled children. Although he vehemently denied it, Natasha couldn't help but believe he was a member of the flourishing Asian sex tourism trade. Despite his denials, she wanted out of the marriage, and out she got, taking the house (and almost all its contents), three cars, a hefty settlement, and extremely large monthly child support checks.

*He was left with half a fortune. But to hear him tell it, he had to start building his business over again from scratch. He was furious. He couldn't remember what he ever saw in her. To his friends she became known as "TFC" (That Fucking Cunt).*

*Did she care? Not one bit. The sting of betrayal enabled her to move on without looking back. TFC was determined to start over. She left the state, sent her kids to European boarding school, renovated her look, and found a filthy rich older man who thought Natasha was his dream-come-true. Although her new husband is confined to a wheelchair much of the time, Natasha makes him feel young again. She's always careful to be extra courteous to his adult children, who eventually developed a grudging respect for the way she treats their dad.*

*Now TFC is filthy rich. Her children have received the finest education and they each speak three languages. They're grateful their mother cared enough about them to provide such an enriching environment. As for Natasha, she hosts fabulous parties and has developed a powerful social network. Most importantly, she found out early that romantic love is fleeting; in fact, she stopped believing in it. She rededicated herself to her children, herself, and her new family. But most important of all, she is blissfully happy.*

TFC turned out to be a natural gold-digger. When Natasha's mother told her she wanted a better life for her, Natasha took it seriously. In her youth, she wanted to combine money with love, but she quickly became disillusioned by what had once felt like love—that feeling soon vanished with loneliness and her husband's insatiable sexual appetites. What she found had lasted was the money she got out of the marriage. But most modern women might look down on Natasha's actions. She didn't look for love the second time around; she looked for something bankable. She transformed herself into an old fashioned gold-digger. Currently, our society looks down on this once time-honored tradition, but it's high time we rethink this disdain for women who evolve from sappy to savvy.

Unlike men who, across many cultures, want young hotties, women aren't as rigid in their preferences. Anthropologist David Buss found women have a slight preference for a strong male provider, but he also found vast inconsistencies.[46] Indeed, many modern women today seek partners without any financial considerations at all, according to Meredith Small, Professor of Anthropology at Cornell University.[47] Our survey of women in their twenties revealed that most have *no preference* for a man with money over a broke-dick dog. Some girls even said that they could go for a subordinate "if he was cute."

So at the same time societal norms condemn us for look-ing for a man with resources, they encourage and reward men who go after a woman for *her* resources: her figure and her fertility. These days we girls have to be fit, femme, and fuckable. And if we're not "super hot," peer pressure and impossible beauty standards make many men (and even other gals) feel free to criticize and demean us for failing to achieve their ideals.

> ### GOLD-DIGGING GIRL QUOTE
>
> Women want mediocre men and men are working to be as mediocre as possible.
>
> *Margaret Mead, Cultural Anthropologist*

There's an obvious imbalance here. While we girls are demanding less and less from men, men are demanding more from us. We've allowed them to drop the ball on their time-honored obligation to provide for their women (and chil-dren). They don't mind sending their girlfriends and wives toddling off to work in a tight skirt and stilettos while they schlep to the basement in their baggy pants to play video games, surf the net, or work on the next great invention. Why do women put up with it?

Our modern spin on gold-digging should be viewed as the new morality: a helpful way for men to rediscover their innate manliness. It's a course correction that will prevent us from veering off the cliff into a world where women work hard, look good, develop a wrinkle and then get tossed out like yesterday's garbage. While it may be news to smart girls, most bimbos already had a clue, probably because they had no other cards to play. It's time to show them all who the real card sharks are.

## BOTTOM LINE

Gold-digging is good for both you and mankind.

## CHAPTER 19

# Fabulous, but Foolish

*Experience is the name everyone
gives to their mistakes.*

OSCAR WILDE, WRITER

By now we've established that young women are the proud owners of unstoppable sexual power. Sure, some of us are more beautiful than others, and certainly innumerable benefits accrue to those who are *exceptionally* good-looking. Dr. Nancy Etcoff wrote a book on the subject, *Survival of the Prettiest*, which highlights a few of these findings[48] that are well-known to many of us.

- People will help a beautiful girl even if they don't like her.
- Good-looking people are less likely to be asked to help others.
- In the workplace, pretty women are more likely to be hired.
- Attractive men and women are given more personal space.

• Gorgeous individuals of both sexes demand and get better service.

But here's the funny thing: despite all these advantages, even if you are magnificently gorgeous and you know it, you can still blow it. Helen learned the hard way.

## ...but Never a Bride

*Helen was a dazzling glamour girl. She spoke five languages fluently and had a beauty so startling that men chased her in droves.*

*"I used to feel sorry for her boyfriends," her brother admitted. "She treated them terribly."*

*And still they kept coming. Her combination of beauty and her bitchiness kept them entranced. Her friends soon grew jealous of her many travel invitations. She spent her summers in Positano when it was still a sleepy little Italian seaside village known only to fishermen and rich Italians. She spent winter holidays in Alpine chalets, spring times in Paris.*

*Although she was a "nobody"—her family could claim neither wealth nor status— while still in her teens Helen began to keep company with the children of European millionaires and minor aristocracy.*

*Soon, she had marriage proposals by the dozens.*

*But she sought love. (See Chapter Seven.)*

*She turned down a marriage offer from a Roman noble, because something about him was distasteful. She cannot now remember what it was.*

*She turned down an offer from a wealthy Greek industrialist. "Too crass," was her reason. "Greeks have no culture." (Girlfriend, please!!)*

*The list is extensive— of both suitors and her reasons for rejecting them. She made the mistake of many who are blessed with beauty—she believed that it was an unshakable part of who she was. She just knew that she would always be desired.*

*As she aged her looks hardened. And she was still a bitch, so she was no longer wooed. She ended up consorting with the valet at the Bel Air Hotel, where she was working as a shop clerk.*

*She found herself pregnant.*

*And then she found herself alone and abandoned with a baby girl.*

*Now pushing 50, Helen is still attractive and lithe, but her face is lined with grief and loneliness. She laughs bitterly at even the thought of going out on a date.*

*Despite being frugal, with no formal education, Helen works menial jobs, and her excess income goes to her daughter's private school tuition. She counsels her daughter not to repeat her foolish mistakes.*

Helen might have exchanged her youth and beauty for the title of an aristocrat or for wealth. Instead of a lifetime of comfort and joy, she rejected a multitude of good offers, squandered her beauty, and ended up with a life that very few people would envy.

### GOLD-DIGGING GIRL QUOTE

Catered to all of their lives, beauties become convinced that they can get whatever they want and whomever they want, a stance bound to lead to frustration.

*Edith Jacobson, Psychoanalyst*

Extraordinary beauties can lose perspective on the big picture because of the distorted lens through which they view the world. Combined with the arrogance of youth, their hotness itself can impede them. They may end up dropping the ball when they could have had an easy score.

### BOTTOM LINE

Don't waste time wishing you were something you're not. Exquisite beauty offers no guarantees. So put down that fashion rag and go dig for gold.

**CHAPTER 20**

# Finding Fidelity

*Getting divorced just because you don't love a man is almost as silly as getting married just because you do.*

EVA GABOR, ACTRESS

We know a girl named Annette who paid an enormous sum to find a date through a high-end matchmaking service. They set her up with ten partners, all attractive and well-mannered. She rejected six and the other four rejected her. Of the ten dates, neither of the pair agreed to try again. After just a single lunch, one or the other decided the spark was not there.

Why?

Attraction seems to be related to the invisible chemical messages the body exudes in the form of pheromones. Unfortunately, most of the science on pheromones has been done on lower animals and has little application to us. These studies often run to the absurd: the regularizing of women's periods when they sniff men's armpit sweat, or the almost totally unrelated work on the sex life of cockroaches.[49] Let's get real: if the best that all this research can come up with is Chaps for Men, we're a long, long way from understanding the rules of attraction.

Another woman we know named Claire used the same matchmaking service that Annette had tried. Her first date was, she said, "just okay." No spark, per se, but he was cute, nice enough and paid for dinner, so she decided to go out on a second date. By the third date, they discovered they had quite a few things in common. By date six they were talking about their finances, families and foibles. Three months into the relationship they were looking at rings. They both agree that the exorbitant fee they paid to meet was well worth it.

Science and psychology have come up with a few answers about forming attachments—if only you can make it through a few dates. Here's a story from our friend Loretta.

## Swaying the Course

*Loretta worked with Andre, an up-and-comer at a hip management consulting company. They traveled out of town together during the week, and when back in Dallas for the week-*

ends, she struggled to find a worthy playmate, while he quickly found himself involved with a beautiful young woman named Katie. Andre and Loretta were "just friends," but the sexual tension between them led to one or two indiscretions.

Loretta met Katie on several occasions and found her sullen and dull. She hated saying it to Andre, but she really didn't like the girl.

He turned to Loretta with his wise, kind eyes and said, "I know what you mean. I don't think I like her, either."

But over the next year and a half as a high-flying consultant Andre would jet to Europe during the week and would come home exhausted, too fatigued to look for someone else. He was short on time and long on lust, so each weekend, he'd grab some flowers on his way home to Katie, who was waiting for him with her legs akimbo. Before he knew it he was falling in love. (See Chapter Seven.)

"I'm damn near married!" he exclaimed to Loretta one day. She replied with a disapproving silence.

"I swear," he commented, "she gives me head that's off the hinges!"

Loretta was "too busy" to attend their black-tie wedding.

Two years later, when Loretta called Andre to wish him a happy birthday he said, "I have news."

A pause. Then, "Let me shut my door so my assistant doesn't hear."

*Loretta was intrigued.*

*"I'm getting divorced," he said with bitterness in his voice.*

*"No!" Loretta said, much-surprised and a bit confused. "What happened?"*

*Andre said, "Katie was like, 'Why aren't you romancing me anymore?' and I was like, 'I work 14 hours a day, I'm exhausted,' and she couldn't put up with it and she kicked me out! Of my own house!"*

*"Is she robbing you?" Loretta asked knowingly.*

*"Yes," he sighed. "She is."*

Now this is what we call a gold-digging success story. Katie, another natural born gold-digger, ended up with a house of her own *and* she also scored almost a million bucks on top of that. She was rich and she hadn't yet turned 30. A chick like that has something to teach all of us. How exactly did this unpleasant and unemployed woman achieve financial freedom?

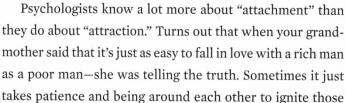

Psychologists know a lot more about "attachment" than they do about "attraction." Turns out that when your grandmother said that it's just as easy to fall in love with a rich man as a poor man—she was telling the truth. Sometimes it just takes patience and being around each other to ignite those feelings that at first might seem lacking.

Take arranged marriages, for example. In many cultures mom and dad (and money and social standing) decide who marries. And you know what? A lot of those marriages last and thrive and the couples even "fall in love."

In Theresa Crenshaw's book *The Alchemy of Love* she notes that when two people touch their bond becomes stronger. Being held can create the illusion of protection and security. That may be why we are so prone to getting bonded to Mr. Wrong: After all, even snakes cuddle.

So here's a tip: being nearby can lead to the physical intimacy that activates the biochemical reaction commonly referred to as "love." Then, like Katie, who just hung on and held tight, you too can be set for life.

———— ∞∞∞ ————

Sound too good to be true? Not in our experience. The story of our friend Rachel, who lost out to a practitioner of the fine art of tenacity is a case in point.

## Old Faithful

*Rachel met Peter in her study group in graduate school. He charmed her with his wit. She hypnotized him with her gorgeous body and an uncanny ability to take classroom notes while simultaneously sending sexy text messages. Peter was engaged to marry a girl named Dixie.*

*Nonetheless, Rachel and Peter were ending each study session with wild sex romps. One day while walking down College Avenue, she blurted out, "Don't marry her, marry me!"*

*Peter stopped and looked at her. When their eyes locked they were transported, floating above the earth, their loins hot with passion. "You're right. We're made for each other. But, how did this happen so fast?"*

*They admitted that their love had come down upon them swiftly. But in her late twenties this was the first time Rachel had ever felt this way. This was what the fairytales had been about. This was love and this was better than anything. Except when he was with his fiancée, at which times Rachel drank copious amounts of red table wine and cried until she vomited.*

*Aggrieved, Rachel asked "How did you two ever end up together?"*

*"It's hard to explain," he said. "I couldn't get rid of her. Then I kind of got used to her."*

———— ⚮ ————

This was pure chemistry at work. Peter said he never even liked his fiancée. In short, Dixie had arranged her own marriage. She had a handsome man with a fat income and decided it was a match, even if he disagreed.

We believe this tradition of arranging your own marriage should be revived. Ladies, we estimate that a girl has about fifteen golden years to catch a big fish and arrange a marriage to the man of her dreams so she can make it to the Promised Land.

But let's finish Rachel's story. It gets a little kinky.

## Three's a Crowd

*Peter and Rachel parted the following summer after being awarded internships in different cities. During their separation, Peter changed his mind again and decided Rachel really was the woman he loved. He went home and told Dixie he wanted to postpone the wedding.*

*But Dixie stood her ground. She too was in love and wasn't about to step aside. She blubbered and begged and badgered him until finally Peter caved in. He married her in a private family ceremony on the Georgia coast. Rachel was devastated. Dixie had gotten her man. Or so it seemed.*

*Three months later, Peter and Rachel ran into each other and once again it was ON. After a lifetime of searching, Rachel believed she had found what she'd always wanted—"true love."*

*Drunk with passion, they continued their afternoon trysts until one day it occurred to Rachel that Peter hadn't yet told Dixie of his unfortunate mistake in accidentally marrying the wrong woman.*

*"I'm afraid to leave her," he said, "You should have seen how broken she was when I told her I wasn't going through with the wedding. She told me she could never get over it."*

*Rachel was in so deep all rational thought was abandoned. She craved his time and attention like an addict hooked on crack. In her heart of hearts, she knew he would ultimately make the right decision by leaving Dixie and coming "home" where he belonged.*

*But then something unexpected occurred. Because they lived in the same condo complex, Rachel got to know Peter's wife Dixie and began to feel guilty about the affair. So Peter came up with an unconventional proposal: They'd all have sex together.*

*And they did. All three. A regular ménage-a-trois.*

*Rachel and Dixie, both wasted on the love drug, shared their man in a way they'd never imagined possible.*

*The following spring, Rachel and Peter managed to sneak off for one last romantic weekend together—just the two of them for a change. And while they lay in bed in an ocean-front hotel room overlooking Stinson Beach, Rachel told Peter to make a decision.*

*"I love you. I really do," he said, laying his head on her breast. "And I don't even like Dixie. But she loves me. And I can't leave."*

*And he didn't.*

Why did Peter stay with Dixie? The two of them went on to save their marriage and have children and live well. Dixie's biggest hobby nowadays is constantly updating her family's online blog. What was Peter thinking? Was it cowardice? Did he cast his lot with the wrong woman? Or is this what fidelity looks like stripped of its handsome mask of morality? After a little thought, it turns out, we don't really care. We're more interested in the girls in this story.

It's actually Dixie who should be examined. She was the one who bore the humiliation of having her big wedding cancelled, sat by while the two of them mooned at each other across their dining room table, then actually joined her competitor in bed with her own husband!

But Dixie hung on. She knew what she wanted. She dug in her nails, convinced him to stay, and she won.

## BOTTOM LINE

Arrange your own marriage. If you're sure your mate is a match you can live with and that he will provide, fight like hell for the marriage you want.

**CHAPTER 21**

# Facelift: Gold-Digging After 40

*You can't turn back the clock.
But you can wind it up again.*

BONNIE PRUDDEN, ATHLETE/AUTHOR

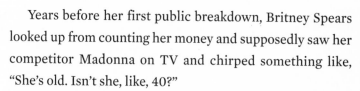

Years before her first public breakdown, Britney Spears looked up from counting her money and supposedly saw her competitor Madonna on TV and chirped something like, "She's old. Isn't she, like, 40?"

The comparatively wise Material Girl told the press, "One day Britney will be as old as her parents, too." That is, if she's lucky.

We all seem to stress out over our cultural obsession with youth and hotness. Although in general we try not to whine (not very hard), we do think it's unfair that just as we girls start getting jowly and receiving (undeserved) dismissive glances, our male contemporaries start getting jowly and acquiring (undeserved) admiring girlfriends.

We can say for certain that we don't want to be men. But once again we find ourselves quoting Maureen Dowd. "We'd like to be like men in the way that they can look good in many different ways [as they age], whereas women are expected to endlessly replicate themselves at twenty-five a la Goldie Hawn and Heather Locklear . . . until they look like frozen reproductions of themselves."

It sucks that men don't appreciate our crow's feet, but usually they don't.

If you're old, or feel old, you may be convinced it's too late. But don't let the societal preoccupation with youth get you down. Slowing, and even reversing, the aging process is now available retail—gym memberships, spa treatments, even vaginal rejuvenation. Hell, we don't care if you suck the fat out of your ass and use it to plump up your tits. Whatever makes you feel beautiful, go for it.

So even if your original sell-by date is long overdue, you may still avoid working until you drop dead. While our shout-out is primarily for the young supple beauties squandering their hotness—if you're older and you aren't married to a man with money, there's still time.

A case in point: At 48, actress Ellen Barkin married one of the richest men in the world. True, it didn't work out, but five years later the rumored $60 million divorce settlement might have taken out just a little bit of the sting. Not to mention that she auctioned off all the jewels he had given her—how satisfying.

Other fun celebrity hook ups include Helen Mirren and hunky younger hubby Taylor Hackford (married in their fifties), Ralph Fiennes and elegant Francesca Annis (she's 18 years older than he is) and *Desperate Housewives'* Marcia Cross, who married in her forties and immediately popped out beautiful twins.

Okay, sure, those ladies are all actresses with fabulous stylists and obsequious personal assistants. With all these people at their beck and call, of course they have time and energy to get facial peels, personalized Pilates lessons and cellulite treatments by beefy-armed Russian women who treat them badly. But what about the average Jane?

Well, just look around, being over 40 is now a brave new world. First of all, we older gals are looking better than ever—the cliché that 40 is the new 30 is true. And when it comes to landing a man, there are numerous advantages to being sexually experienced. Plus, older women don't bring the same pressures to a new relationship because they don't have that desperate worry about how it's all going to work out.

The older woman "is less likely to have an agenda . . . no biological clock tick-tocking beside her lover's bed, no campaign to lead him to the altar, no rescue fantasies," says author Gail Sheehy in *Sex and the Seasoned Woman*.[50] (And if you do have a campaign to lead him to the altar, keep it to yourself.)

The old line that women who delay marriage won't ever get married is simply no longer true. "More women now marry for the first time in their forties, fifties and even sixties now than ever before," says marriage historian Stephanie Coontz. Another cool point Coontz raises, "Women are now willing to marry younger men and younger men are now more willing to marry them." All this good news seems to run contrary to our dominant "youth conquers all" culture, so lucky for us every cloud has a silver-haired lining. Just go ask Alice.

## Fuck Yoga

*At a yoga retreat in the mountains above Santa Barbara, everyone was a bit surprised when Alice, a weekend yoga instructor, showed up with her new husband, Victor. He looked much younger than she, and was a gorgeous specimen of blond, muscled lusciousness.*

*"Is he her son?" someone whispered.*

*Alice, 45, had worked as a marketing analyst but was unful-filled. She invested her savings in a two-week yoga teacher's workshop to refresh and relax. She was a kind, elegant woman but not especially beautiful, though her yoga practice gave her a fit, flexible body.*

*Alice completed her training and then started teaching classes in her hometown and loved it, though her paycheck was much smaller. Then she met a new student named Victor. At first she treated him in a motherly way, never thinking she would be on his sexual radar. But it wasn't long before the two were a couple. He had a great job and loved taking care of Alice. They married, and now she takes care of him, too, though he pays the bills. Alice teaches yoga on the side. After five years, they're still going strong. A match made in Nirvana.*

---

Okay, so you may be thinking, "That's fine for Alice, but I'm no yogi." Perhaps you're envisioning Tantric sex positions, a taut yoga bod and flexibility you just don't have. It may just sound painful and exhausting.

Why shouldn't we have self-doubt? Most of us are under the spell of the non-stop media assault on our body image, especially as we age. Historically, one of the problems for us older girls has been a lack of positive role models.

But things are changing slowly for the better. Women like Oprah Winfrey and Susan Sarandon have shown grace as they have aged in the public eye. In fact, at 50-plus they look better than ever and they don't look like girls. They don't look like they are trying to be twenty. They look like mature, confident women.

Marketers have also jumped on the over-40 bandwagon. Pond's launched an ad campaign called, "The Other Side of 40," that featured orgasmically happy older women walking down city streets while chuckling as they watch men gaze at the asses of younger women in higher heels. There's even a successful monthly magazine, *More*, dedicated to the still vital over-40 woman—and it's just as much *Glamour* as it is *Prevention*. "It's never too late to age well," they say.

On the other hand, Nora Ephron, a brilliant screenwriter, producer and director, wants to be free to complain about the "ravages" of aging and does so in an amusing way in her book *I Feel Bad About My Neck: And Other Thoughts on Being a Woman*. She's got money, friends and talent, but she really wishes she'd spent more time in her youth just admiring her neck. When Ms. Ephron was interviewed about her book, she complained that no one ever told her about getting old, and bemoaned the fact that she had grown a mustache. It's diverting, but researchers say if we spend less time on self-slander, we'll look better as the years roll by.

A study from the Yale School of Public Health[51] has shown that positive perceptions of aging increase longevity even more than low weight, good blood pressure and not smoking.

So when you call that brain freeze a "senior moment" you may be doing more harm than you think. When you spend too much time whining about new wrinkles, you may actually sprout a few new gray hairs for your trouble. The research says to reframe your reality and embrace this paradox: Sincerely looking forward to getting older helps you stay younger.

So Nora, honestly, your neck looks great in that scarf.

If you've already squandered your youthful nubility, all is not lost. It may be true that your eggs are no longer viable and that some men are no longer an option—but there are many others who are. With age comes confidence. No longer needy and desperate for male attention, an older woman has a different kind of power than she had when she was younger. She may have her own career, her own condo and a couple of bucks of her own in the bank. However, this doesn't mean that a grown-up woman should pay the bills for her man just to have him in the picture.

So whether you just never got around to it or couldn't find "true love" up to now, never fear, marriage is still an option and financial security should factor into that deal. But we're sticking by the GDI and will make one thing perfectly clear: Unless you are already rich, when looking for a matrimonial partner, you need to look deeper, and check for deep pockets.

Knowing a bit about the world and what makes men tick gives silver sirens a leg up to getting their legs wrapped around a man with cash. It's just not the exact *same* one you might have taken up with 20 years ago. And that's not always a bad thing.

## BOTTOM LINE

Finding a mate is possible at any age, but
don't forget to dig for gold.

**CHAPTER 22**

# 411: How to Score a Man with Money

*The rich have to marry someone, why not you?*

GINIE POLO SAYLES, AUTHOR

As you read this, you may be mumbling to yourself, "I can't even get a decent date, let alone a rich one."

Point taken. This book was never intended to be a how-to guide. There are already scores of books dedicated solely to teaching you how and where to hunt the rich. For those unfamiliar with these books, the advice seems to come straight from Marketing 101: Price, Product, Placement, and Positioning.

**Price.** Come to terms with how rich you want to be and start keeping an eye out for your earner. Keep that number in your mind when looking for a husband, but also remember the character traits you can and cannot abide. All the gold-digging guides agree: the highest price to pay is ending up living with someone you despise. Once you have a mental picture of your "Prince," get to work imagining your new life. The law of attraction will bring it to you. This has to be true, we saw it on Oprah.

**Product.** You're the product and you must invest in making yourself the best you can be. Again, all the guides agree: Be clean, wear make-up and dress your best at all times. Some of these books send you to thrift shops and e-Bay to dress well on a budget. Eat healthy foods. Work out and take vitamins so your hair, skin and attitude will be top-notch. Start investing small sums in the stock market so you can see your actual worth building. If you say you don't have the cash, use the money you're thinking of spending on a therapist (mental health: so illusory, so overrated). One of the most entertaining gold-digging guides, *How to Marry a Multi-Millionaire*, takes the idea of improving "the product" a bit over the top with advice like take up smoking, ingest amphetamines, and do at least 3 to 5 hours of cardio a day. Their motto: you are never too thin unless you're invisible when you're standing sideways.

**Placement.** Place yourself in the way of the rich. Go ahead and take a little survey of the people that are in your life. How did you meet them? The rule of love and friendship is governed by proximity. Volunteer for a medical charity or an upscale political group, go to auctions, visit a posh resort, go on a cruise. Move into a wealthy neighborhood. As Aristotle Onassis said, "If you want to be rich, live with the rich, even if you have to live in the attic." Ginie Polo Sayles, world-renowned expert on "The Rich," even suggests techniques that border on stalking, like following a high end car to the coffee shop so you can pretend "fate" brought you together.

> **GOLD-DIGGING GIRL TIP**
>
> Eighty percent of the people who get married live within two miles of each other.
>
> *Dr. Joyce Brothers*

Experts on grabbing a rich husband also say . . . get a job! Some jobs put you in proximity to the wealthy: nannies (Robin Williams married his); bartenders (Matt Damon married his); personal assistants (Christian Bale married someone else's); realtors (get to sell houses to rich people); journalists (get to interview celebrities); shop clerks in expensive stores (*Shopgirl*, we're not sure this counts).

Attend charity events and art openings, movie premieres and the opera. Try not to break your bank attending these high-end affairs—sneaking in can be fun and free. (Our friend Camilla frequently goes to Will-Call demanding seats she never ordered. After mercilessly badgering the bewildered box office agent, she often ends up sitting front-row center.) Consider learning the rules of polo, but remember that a lot of (especially nouveau) rich guys like football—just like the Joe Six-Pack who still owes you money for gas.

**Positioning.** This has to do with how you want the rich to see you: the Smart Girl, the Sporty Girl, the Horsewoman, etc. It also means what you do with your time, what your hobbies and interests are—in other words, the total package. So when you come down from your attic and out into public, pretend you're already rich. Pass the afternoon in beautiful places. The available guides give some very specific and often hilarious info on how to walk (poise, ladies, poise!), what to wear (only white shirts and tailored skirts!), what to cook (use exquisite garnishes!), and even how to decorate your apartment (tiny guest soaps in the bathroom!).

As you mince delicately down the street with your head held high looking for tiny soaps, the guides recommend simply loitering around high-end shopping areas or having a coffee at a fine restaurant. Not only will this realign your awareness with the finest things in life, but you might also meet someone with money.

As you enter a relationship and begin to weigh the pros and cons of personality, sexuality and other considerations, always remember this: Follow the money. Ginie Polo Sayles says it well, "If a Rich Man tells you he loves you, but doesn't spend money on you, it's a lie . . . Money-spending is one of the greatest indicators of love."

## The Rules

Another resource that many women have opted for as they look for a mate is a best-selling book that came out in the 1990s called *The Rules*. This earnest paperback resonated with women who all secretly wish for the magic power to find their Prince Charming. The book promises to teach you *the* way to find *the* guy—not just one with cash but your actual soul mate. One of the authors ultimately divorced her husband, but whatever.

*The Rules'* secret is mostly about playing hard to get, waiting to reveal your true self to a man and above all NOT answering the phone. It's kind of a mirror image of another bestseller *He's Not That Into You*, wherein the authors basically say that if a man doesn't call, walk away. As far as *The Rules* goes, we've known many women who have followed the recipe step-by-step and won. In our experience, just working

*The Rules* can be a form of discipline that can keep a smart girl from falling in love with the wrong guy.

One of the rules is that you're supposed to hold off having sex for specific amounts of time, depending on your age. We're fairly sure your mother said something about "why buy the cow when you can get the milk for free?" You probably weren't listening. In fact, many women we know have sex on the first date routinely, so they can know what they are getting into. Our lusty friend Nicole calls it a "test drive."

If you're extremely sexual, it may not be a bad way to go, although we think men are educable in this area. Nevertheless, we have a friend who is currently married to her third (wealthy) husband who off-handedly admitted to us, "Oh, I fucked all my husbands on the first date." Now *there's* a statement that speaks for itself.

At any rate, many girls we know break *The Rules* routinely and still wind up with the guy. Anastasia just didn't have the willpower to stay away from the telephone.

## Thank You for Calling

*Anastasia was a simple girl with a pretentious name that didn't suit her. She was not that smart and made little sense in conversation, but she was gifted with a photographic memory. Her enormous capacity to regurgitate educational material propelled her into the legal profession.*

*While in law school, she met Tony, who was visiting her classmate Jim. Tony was a dreamboat. He had big, soulful blue eyes and was a Brad Pitt look-alike who played guitar and sang. He was also a financially well-off geek renowned for some top-notch computer games he had programmed.*

*He was THE ONE, at least in Anastasia's mind, so she went to work. She played coy and aggressive. She was cute and gazed up at him while he strummed and sang. Tony loved the adoration. Deep down he was a shy guy who, despite his good looks, had never been comfortable approaching girls. He'd never needed such skills, as the modern liberated woman came to him.*

*Breaking every rule in the art of trapping a man, Anastasia slept with him that same night. And the next. And the next. Then he went back to Boston and she never heard from him again. She was beside herself—she had fallen in love (See Chapter Seven).*

*Her friend Jim was blunt. "You should never have slept with him. He's got dozens of girls. He's not going to call."*

*And he didn't.*

*But she did.*

*And did. And did. And did. And then the phone sex started, and before he knew it Tony was hooked. And then he was buying plane tickets. And she was coming up for the weekends. For eight long years they sustained this. And then they married. And they had babies. And though they have some wicked fights, they are still together as of press time.*

In any event, he makes good money and they have no pre-nup, so if and when he or she walks, at least she won't end up having to work until the end of her days.

Our point is this: Read the books and follow the advice to the degree you can. *How to Marry a Multi Millionaire* insists you *must* move to Manhattan if you are really serious about digging for the kind of gold that's worth digging for. Others can find gold in aisle 14B at the hardware store in any Small Town, USA. Find your own style of fishing for fortune, then shop carefully.

### BOTTOM LINE

There's a rich guy out there for everyone. After all, they often circle back once or twice for new brides.

## CHAPTER 23

# Financial Freak Out

**_Women can invest, save and handle debt just as well and skillfully as any man. Why would anyone think otherwise?_**

SUZE ORMON, FINANCIAL GURU

Even if you already have a personal shopper on speed dial or you're sitting on a private jet whisking you to Napa right now, you still can't just leave all the financial planning and organization up to a man. Every one of us needs to focus on the money. This is the great dividing line that separates smart girls from the rest. So you gotta get a grip.

## A Girl We Know

_Stella is a married woman who runs her own endowment fund. She raises and invests millions of dollars every month. But she's in trouble with her student loans and has a credit card her_

*husband knows nothing about, with a balance of almost $25,000.*
*She actually has the cash in her personal investment account to*
*clear the card, but for some unknown reason she just ignores it.*

In 2007, financial guru Suze Ormon hit a nerve with her eighth book, *Women and Money*. Up to that point, Ormon focused on basic financial strategies with no emphasis on either gender. Then she noticed a disturbing trend of women actively ignoring their own financial welfare. She noted that these gals were "clueless . . . or in some cases willingly resisting doing what they [needed to do]."

The big surprise to Ormon was that these were "smart, competent, accomplished women," not silly, self-absorbed nitwits. She dug a little deeper and found that even some of her closest girlfriends were hiding their fear of finances. Ormon has dubbed it, "the *unknown factor* that prevents them from doing the right thing with their money."

## A Girl We Know About

*Terri is a single girl who works as an actress and leases a sweet BMW. She hasn't paid personal income taxes in three years. She says she's just "running late." She has kept virtually no records of her various jobs and has no idea where to begin. All those numbers make her feel dizzy. She is, however, impeccably groomed and usually well-organized. She hasn't missed her scheduled Thursday manicure in seven years.*

Maybe for some women it's a fear of the unknown; Ormon wonders if maybe it isn't a little streak of rebellion for holding it together in every other part of their lives. Or perhaps it's just that things had gotten so far out of hand, they're embarrassed.

Ormon must've struck upon something because her book sold like hotcakes. Could it be that more than a few gals are struggling to get over this *"unknown factor"*? Suze Ormon's popularity has helped propel her to the kind of international celebrity seldom bestowed upon financial advisors. She now has her own talk show and has been named one of *Time Magazine's* Top 100 Most Influential People.

## A Girl We Didn't Know

*She was an heiress. She grew up spoiled by opulence, learning all the rules of etiquette but none of balancing a checkbook. Towards the end of her life, she lived in a hotel, where stalkers would snatch her jewels while she sat in the lounge. She had once been one of the richest women on earth. She died with just $3,000 in the bank. Her name was Barbara Hutton, heir to the Woolworth fortune.*

Barbara Hutton died nearly penniless in 1979. Although she inherited a huge fortune, she was not given the skills to manage that money. She was a victim of the age-old prejudice that women shouldn't or are unable to handle money.

This let her fall victim to gold-digging men and serious financial mismanagement.

But these days, all women have access to a variety of financial resources from books and online tools, to seminars and investing clubs. And for those who are still intimidated there are even guides for Idiots *and* Dummies.

We girls need to be financially savvy in all economic climates, but especially now. Sure we know there are plenty of women who have their act together when it comes to money management. (Y'all can skip this part and jump back to the orgasm chapter.) But for the rest of us, like going to the gym or wearing moisturizer, this is one of those things a smart girl simply must do.

## Another Girl We Know

*Sonia was a youthful 37-year-old who made a decent living as a freelance commercial casting agent. However, her love of the finer things in life kept her on the verge of bankruptcy. When one employer discovered an accounting error, she received a fat check. She was ecstatic. We all thought she would clear her credit cards and back rent and move forward. Instead she went to Dubai for a week because she heard it had the best shopping venues in the world. Sure, she had the time of her life, but when she got back to face the bills, she wondered aloud why her financial karma just never seemed to change.*

We are not financial counselors any more than we are matchmakers, but we've discovered that there are so many helpful resources available that there's no excuse to keep dragging yourself further into debt. If you spend a little time working on it, you can probably find a resource that works for you.

Overall, there's some agreement as to the basics. The gurus of dollars and sense want you to ask yourself: have you ever created a true budget, including one-time splurges, divided by 12? (Ouch!) Have you paid off your high interest rate credit cards? Have you purchased proper health, life, or car insurance? And that's just the beginning.

If you've never done any of these things, it's time to switch into high gear. This means putting these money matters at the top of your priority list instead of continuing to ignore them. Ormon has a whole "survival" method that makes sense, so if you find yourself completely at a loss, perhaps you should start with her book, or at least hit her website.

*Working Women's Magazine* summed up a few of the biggest mistakes the modern gal can make:

- Assuming your current financial situation is permanent
- Not using a budget
- Waiting to save

We know you're smart girls, so after you finish feeling guilty, maybe a little stomach-achey, or if you had chest pains while reading this like we did when we wrote it, now's the time to stop feeling sorry for yourself and get to work. The budget thing is a recurring theme, so start making one—the dry-cleaning can wait. It's a habit that may just change your life forever.

## A Couple We Know

*They were a young professional couple. He was an engineer and she was a young professor teaching comparative religion. The couple bought a tiny condo, but even with their six-figure combined income, they barely made enough to cover the mortgage, pay school loans, and support her mother and their premature twins. When she didn't get tenure, she was asked to leave. She scrambled to get a job. But just what can an out-of-work religion professor do besides teach? She took a job as an administrator twice a week at a methadone clinic, until she could get credentialed to teach at the local high school. She and her husband soon went into the red and were forced to sell their condo in a down-market.*

Unfortunately, just being a successful career gal, a great companion, girlfriend, or hot, hot, hot lover, doesn't secure anything for the modern woman. Plus, many high achievers are hobbled by the Achilles heel of financial fear. Fortunately, it's fixable, and you don't need to visit an orthopedic surgeon.

If more women took time to learn a bit more about money, we think the numbers in the big picture would change, especially in terms of "older girls" and retirement. After all, since we now know that women live longer and make less money than men, it makes sense that we should budget, save and invest more aggressively than men. It's time to get on it.

> **GOLD-DIGGING GIRL QUOTE**
>
> A man is not a financial plan.
>
> *Leslie Bennetts, The Feminine Mistake*

We agree with Bennetts' statement that a man is not a financial plan, but he can be *part of one*. Most of us want to pair up at some point, so we can't forget about the GDI— remember it's the Gold-Digging *Imperative*, which means that you have no choice but to factor in earning power when picking a mate. Use your looks to cash in and then build your wealth.

Don't be fabulous and act foolish because even if you land a big fish, without planning, you may still wake up at middle age alone and with no exit strategy. Now that's not something a smart girl would do, is it?

If and when you make a long-term commitment to someone, learn your guy's financial plan in detail. Even if your golden guy stays with you and is a virtual fountain of financial youth, he might get hit by a truck. Or if you end up fluffing, at least you'll have a few bucks socked away so you don't have to restart from dead zero. Or worse, in debt.

And here's some good news. Our "feminine" qualities—like patience, intuition, and tenacity—are just the traits that make smart gals into great investors.

### BOTTOM LINE

Your financial future belongs to you.

## CHAPTER 24

# Fragile: Being Male in a Man's World

*If women didn't exist, all the money in the world would have no meaning.*

ARISTOTLE ONASSIS

"You girls have no idea how fragile the male ego is," Evan told us after reading a rough draft of this book.

"Who isn't fragile?" we thought, but didn't say. He was our first male reader, so we exchanged glances but kept our thoughts to ourselves.

Our thoughts went something like this: Here we girls are, falling in love perpetually from the onset of menstruation, rejected and heartbroken through most of our teen years, then as women our looks are held up to comparison to freakish supermodels, while as young professionals we continually fail in the male-dominated workplace. But do we complain? No, we suck it up and we soldier on. (Okay, so we complain—*bitterly*—but we won't anymore after we marry money when we are young and then move on with our lives.)

Evan didn't notice the looks we exchanged. He was focused on his own fragility thing—and in discussing it—we knew he was betraying his male brethren. It was a rare opportunity. Although he is a successful writer and film director, he was having trouble getting the words out. We were gentle with him. We reminded ourselves that he has a fragment of a chromosome. We listened intently as he tried to explain that it's not all that easy being a guy, either.

"The male ego," he said with his head in his hands. He then flung his hands out in front of him as if to shake us to our senses. "You have no idea."

Evan seemed basically focused on his luck with girls. He is a 20-something, so, as sexologist Theresa Crenshaw wrote, "[He's] as ill-suited for a relationship as he will ever be." He doesn't know this yet. And like everyone else, he's had his share of hits and misses. But it's the *misses* that preoccupy him.

———— ❧ ————

Although he was at a loss for words, we were not. We had done the research and we'd found out a lot about men. We found that current beauty standards are not only tougher on women, but also tougher on men. Increasingly, men are resorting to plastic surgery to look good. In addition, both men and women are unable to escape our Stone Age preference for men who are tall. And that's not something easily fixed by plastic surgery, not even by a reconstructive surgeon from 90210. These demands on men are clearly out of step with the times. Why in the world would the modern professional man need to stand over six feet tall, have big shoulders or, for that matter, nice buns, especially since he's sitting on them all the time?

### GOLD-DIGGING GIRL FACT

Men are now spending nine and a half billion dollars a year on plastic surgery [and other cosmetics]...to be competitive in the work place, and I think, to be sexually competitive.

*Nancy Etcoff, Survival of the Prettiest*

Since we humans were built to survive a savage world, studying beasts in the wild is as good a way as any to help us understand our own biological impulses. Professor Nancy Etcoff reminds us that the most dominant males in animal herds are those that are more warlike, with the largest antlers, tusks, muscles, and physical prowess.

"Male beauty in all species has evolved in large part for male appraisal," Etcoff wrote. A male in a social group who is dominating other males has "proven" he has the best genetic material, and he becomes more attractive to females. Applied to humans, it's an inescapable fact that the respect men show other men is a major factor in attracting women.

By now we know that men and women differ in the basic structure of our cells, our bodies, and our brains. Studies show that an eight-week-old male fetus is already losing brain cells in the centers of communication,[52] while the aggression centers are being super-sized. And while any mom will tell you that male and female toddlers play well together, the minute they hit school age, things start to change.

Boys are tough on each other. Ask anyone who went to an all-male boarding school. He'll tell you that male ranks form quickly amongst boys—within hours. Some magical but instantly recognizable combination of intellect, looks and character (and sometimes wealth) designate dominance. Usually it's the best-looking and most athletic boy who becomes the alpha, while the beta boys fall into rapid formation around him. But if a boy looks like an alpha and proves himself *not to be one*, he is treated cruelly and often becomes the group's "bitch."[53]

It's no wonder then that men are so fragile.

## Boys Will Be Men: The Enron Phenomenon

Then the boys grow up, passing through the rites of the teen years to become well-behaved, egalitarian men who believe in meritocracy and treat everyone fairly. And then we all live happily ever after. Girls, we've warned you about this kind of pixie dust. Before you know it you'll be snorting it up your nose through a straw. Let's take a step back before we all end up in some kind of rehab for the criminally optimistic. Let's look at what really happens when guys write the rules.

Sociologists have observed that in one form or another, men continue to seek the approval of other men pretty much all their lives.[54] How to impress? Hmmm. Plastic surgery might lengthen the male member, but it still can't lengthen the male himself. So just how does a man get another man's respect? Answer: accumulate vast fortune and power.

These days anybody with money never seems to have enough. This colossal greed is a malignant version of the male drive to survive—to look good in other men's eyes. Perhaps reviewing the financial excesses of late, we can take the measure of the modern man. It's an established fact that some businessmen known as "the barons of bankruptcy"❤ made off with some serious loot while their companies like Enron and Worldcom tanked.

Sure, it's old news, but it still matters. One only has to look at the recent explosive events in the mortgage and other financial markets to see where these barons have led us. We had already been "rocked" by so many scandals that we could barely manage a shrug—that is until people lost their homes and watched in horror as their retirement funds dwindled. If we'd been paying attention to financial misdeeds of a few short years ago, these events and the unprecedented bailouts wouldn't have come as such a surprise.

Now we don't even remember the names. We'll try not to bore, but here's a quick summary. In 2001 the Enron brand became synonymous with corporate corruption. And there were many others. But the bottom line was the top *guys* knew their Titanics were sinking and arranged for soothing musical trios to play while their crews lost their shirts, their savings and their lives. (Sound familiar?) Meanwhile the big boys stuffed their pockets and scurried to the lifeboats:

---

❤ So named by *The Financial Times*

- Enron's slippery superintendent slithered off with $250 million
- Global Crossing's oily overseer oozed away with $512 million
- WorldCom's cheating chief checked out with $50 million[55]

For those of us in the middle class (and we count in this category anyone who is worried about covering their monthly nut), we scratch our heads in wonder—why bother lying, cheating and stealing when you already have millions in the bank? A few insider trades and these head honchos could still have packed their purses—and their first and second wives' purses, too. (Don't kid yourselves—it happens every day.) Sure, it didn't work out so well for Martha Stewart, but on the other hand, she doesn't have a penis.

**GOLD-DIGGING GIRL FACT**

In one year alone, Michael Eisner, the soon-to-be ousted head of Walt Disney, cashed in $517 million in stock options.

*The New Yorker Magazine*[56]

With the advent of employee stock options, greed simply exploded. "It became a competitive game to see how much money you could get," the former chairman of the Federal Reserve Board Paul Volcker was quoted as saying in The *New Yorker*.[57] Volcker added, "Traditional norms didn't exist. You had this whole culture where the only *sign of worth* was how much money you made."

Whoa!

Wait up a minute. A few million bucks are enough for even the greediest gold-digger. This man-show wasn't about attracting girls through an updated, yet still primitive mating ritual. It turned into a ritual of an entirely different sort: pure man-on-man action that brought financial ruin to thousands of hard-working families.

---

There's no getting around it: *This Greed Cycle*[58] was created by men, for men. As we've noted before, if even a few women are added to a large group of men, the group's agenda changes to encompass the whole of society, including those who can't speak for themselves. It was, after all, a woman who blew the whistle on Enron.

Why are we going on about this? In part, it's proof that the sexes need each other. If left unchecked, men make the economic world unbalanced. And this is the world of dollars and cents—the one that determines the survival of both sexes in this modern age.

Still you may shrug and say, "Who cares if a few peeps got a pay day?"

Well, it matters. It fucks up the economy. The kinds of fortunes these men made were once reserved for captains of industry and entrepreneurs. These industrious men were rewarded with outsized fortunes for making outsized contributions to society. You might recognize some of them: Rockefeller, Carnegie, Gates, and Jobs, to name a few. But vast fortunes being handed to bureaucrats and middle-managers who steer their companies to disaster has created market distortions that affect all of us. Global Economic Crisis, anyone?

We don't mean to be all pie-in-the-sky, but maybe if more women wielded power at the upper levels there'd be a cultural shift away from the cycle of greed. But even we think it's doubtful as long as women have to use the "be a man strategy" to get ahead.

## BOTTOM LINE

The culture of Boys Nation spurs men to greed,
sometimes to the detriment of society.

## SMART GIRLS' STOCK OPTIONS:
## THE BASICS

Ever wonder how the stock option thing worked? Well, here's pretty much all you need to know. The white collar crooks made their money by creating clandestine schemes worthy of a John Grisham novel. The executives were given the option ("stock option") to buy, say, a million shares of their company stock at perhaps $10 a piece.

This gave the execs serious incentive to drive up the price of their company stock—by any means necessary. But what if the company was doing poorly? No problem. Through accounting artifice and downright deceit they exaggerated income and hid company debts. Successful company hype might send the stock price soaring to $20 a share and ka-ching—overnight the exec would cash out with $10 million.

But if the share price didn't go up, they still got another chance. They could get the company board to give them the right to buy stock at an even lower price, let's say $1.00 a share. So if the price fell to $9 a share, they could still cash out with $8 million. Not a bad bonus for managerial incompetence. One expert remarked, "They created their own money machine . . . a virtual anti-gravity device."

Good for the boys. Bad for the girls. Unless, well, you know . . .

CHAPTER 25

# The Future of Marriage

*The quickest way to conquer
yearning is to yield immediately and move
on to more important things."*

OSCAR WILDE, WRITER

We're fortunate to be living in the information age. For one thing, all the 411 takes the guess work out of what's going on culturally. Although we think we've made a strong case against romantic love, we have to admit that our general fascination with a love story hasn't faded one bit.

As the last millennium closed out, right around the time President Bill Clinton was getting impeached for lying about sexual misconduct, millions lined up to see the movie *Titanic*—a tale of two lovers who met and engaged in . . . sexual misconduct.

We know how the story of Bill and Monica played out, but knowing what we now know, we wondered what would have happened if the Titanic's lovers had both survived.

## Rose's Regrets

*Jack met Rose on the high seas and offered to sketch her portrait—if she would take off all her clothes. Although she was a First Class passenger and he was a ruffian from steerage, she obliged. She knew it was a shipboard romance, so she knew she would go all the way. Besides, there was a new saying that was all the rage: "What happens on The Titanic stays on The Titanic."*

*Rose and Jack had many adventures on the high seas and they were lucky to have both survived the sinking. When she got to New York, Rose had an epiphany. She felt she finally understood that life was fragile, sweet and short and she would no longer deny her profound love for Jack. She decided to take action. The young lovers eloped and quickly tried to put the tragedies behind them.*

*Rose devoted herself to Jack and tried to educate him about art and literature. Oddly, for Jack's part, he quickly lost interest in Rose and her pretensions. He pursued his new myriad interests. He drank liquor daily, bathed rarely and patronized prostitutes regularly.*

*Disenchanted with Jack's lack of ambition and infected with multiple venereal diseases, Rose was soon repulsed by the sight of Jack staggering home drunk and reeking of cheap perfume. It dawned on her that she hadn't been in love, but had suffered a temporary mental derangement heightened by their harrowing brush with death.*

*She pleaded for her mother's help. Since everyone in their New York social set mourned the horrific watery death of Rose's first fiancé Cal, they had written off Rose's elopement with Jack as a grief-driven misjudgment—a misstep that had derailed a once promising life in the New York social scene. An annulment was arranged and Rose soon married a wealthy oil tycoon, who was also very kind and cultured. And he loved Rose's taste in art.*

*Titanic* writer, director, producer and movie-making genius James Cameron came up with the perfect formula for a love story: To keep love alive you must kill it at sea and let the audience wonder what might have been. Cameron, now in his fifth marriage, knew only too well that the sweet cocktail of endless love cannot be made entirely from the bitters of the real world. After all, he is living proof that love is fleeting and marriage, disposable.

Cameron's story made *Titanic* the highest grossing film of all time—worldwide. Movie houses in Japan and India were filled to overflowing. In Taliban-controlled Afghanistan, women risked their lives smuggling bootlegged copies under their burkas. The market had spoken: a good love story is so important to us that we'll take our lives in our hands and spend the last two rupees we have to rub together just to see one. "But," as Stephanie Coontz writes in *The History of Marriage*, "for the most part, our ancestors didn't try to live in one."

Now, of course, it's just the opposite. The cultural expectation is that marriage is based on love and love only. On top of all that, according to Coontz, then we have to cook up an idyllic happy marriage with the following recipe:

1. The couple should choose each other without outside influence.
2. Each partner must love the other deeply and make the other the top priority.
3. Parents and in-laws should not interfere.
4. The couple should express affection openly.
5. And, of course, they should be sexually faithful.

Throughout human history "there have always been happy couples," Coontz writes, "but few have been happy in just this way." Look, even we admit that it's hard to imagine another paradigm. We're all trapped in the same cultural craze for L-O-V-E. But we've got to fight it. We've got to get the facts. And even then, with our heads swimming in romantic ideals, it might seem barbarous that for most of time, marriage has been based on economic, social and political expediencies.

**GOLD-DIGGING GIRL QUOTE**

Marriage was often the only alternative to destitution or prostitution.

*Stephanie Coontz, The History of Marriage*

## Repeating History

Since those who don't know history are doomed to repeat it, let's take a quick tour of marriage through the ages. The ritual of the wedding itself has been astounding in its variations. In the Middle Ages, the European lower classes basically just said, "We're married!" and it was done. Other cultures didn't (and some still don't) require any vows at all: Eating a cooked meal together or staying for breakfast made a pair husband and wife.[59]

There's also this extraordinary ritual—you may have heard of it—when a woman frocks herself in an expensive white ensemble to promenade down a flower-filled aisle of a church that she probably doesn't attend on any regular basis. Afterward the newlyweds fete themselves. They gorge on mediocre food and a mountainous cake with guests they'll likely never see again at a shindig that may very well bankrupt the bride's parents. It is, after all, the happiest day of her life.

The issue of just *who* could marry has been highly regulated. Throughout time and round the world the laws governing eligibility for marriage have ranged widely. In India, two- and three-year-old girls were at one time eligible to be wed. In many parts of the world, 12- and 13-year-olds are still married off in some commercial bargain.[60] (Jail bait? They think not.)

In China, women would often fight over the right to marry a dead relative of an important family in much-coveted "ghost marriages." (This way the woman could stay independent, yet acquire the money and status of her new family.) In a few Native American cultures[61] women have married family pets or, in some cases, a body part, such as a foot. (If you have a fetish for feet, this might be just the arrangement you were looking for—"With this toe ring, I thee wed.")

Let's not forget that through much of time, rigid laws against interracial marriage♥ existed in the West within the living memories of most who are alive today. Although rare, same sex marriages have been permitted in many cultures. But strictures by the church and local cultures made homosexual marriage impossible in the US until recently, and this is still a hotly contested issue.

Laws governing marital rights and relations have taken various forms. Even in the Western world, until recently wives

---

♥ Laws against "miscegenation" in the Southern US were particular strong.

could not hold property in their own name or even get a credit card without their husbands' approval. And although we like to think of ourselves as civilized, throughout much of modern Western history, marital rape and wife beating have been legal. Fast forward to contemporary culture, and we have our own fairly rigid beliefs about marriage: We should fall madly in love (see Chapter Seven) and remain in that state until one of the pair drops dead. Even if we watched our parents bicker and divorce, or witnessed divorces tumble like dominoes through our hometowns, this is still an ideal we in the West hold dear. It's reinforced by the intermittent and highly irritating testimonies of those who claim to be happy in love, have met their soul mates, and are in all other ways better than you.

In our competitive society, this kind of posturing can get on anyone's nerves. Plus, it puts external pressure on women to find "the one." Today, many women let their youth slip away while searching for Mr. Right.

"Somewhere in the world of five billion people there lives the best-looking, richest, smartest, funniest, kindest person who will *settle for you*," wrote Steven Pinker in *How the Mind Works*. As Pinker notes, the problem is basically a sorting issue. How do we find him? We all know the reality: You could croak while you're busy kissing toads.

And taking the time to go around kissing all those toads can be costly. Not only are there the real economic costs of gym memberships, diets, makeup and clothing, there's also loneliness and childlessness, which are costly emotionally.[62] As Pinker notes, "At some point it pays to set up house with the best person you have found so far."

A modern girl confronts this dilemma daily. We've all seen it in the movies: Both women and men fear if they settle they'll miss out on a better opportunity that's bound to be just around the corner. We have the old problem of our inability to foresee our own futures. In a mortal world of imperfect information, it's hard to know what to do. Should we settle for staying single, while looking for "the one"? Or should we settle for someone we're not 100% sure of, believing no one better will come along?

Of course, now we know that love fades and that years down the line you may very well look at the soulmate you held out for and ask yourself, "What the hell was I thinking?" Or do we "settle" for "Mr. He's-better-than-a-kick-in-the-head?" There might just be a middle way: some intermediate course between the search for Mr. Right and the lurch for Mr. Tonight. Let's look at some women's previous solutions and decide.

## Stay Single or Settle?

*"No, I never loved your father,"* Lola said to her daughter, Marian. *"I was afraid I'd never get married. He courted me ferociously—and I kinda felt sorry for him."* This was no surprise to Marian, who had long been bewildered by her parent's

marriage. Sure, on paper even Marian could admit her dad was a catch. But in actuality, Pop had issues. He was often violent, drunk and downright mean.

Since Marian was 15 she had encouraged her mother to leave. When Lola finally did leave, she danced with colorful silk scarves in her new apartment and closed her eyes and planned her new life. At 52, she reasoned, she still had some good years left and a man who caught her interest. Lola was on-top-of-the-world when she called Marian at college to tell her the news. But a few weeks later, a tearful Lola called her husband and begged to come home after the man she was dating told her he was actually looking for someone "quite a bit younger."

**GOLD-DIGGING GIRL QUOTE**

You get what you settle for.

Susan Sarandon, *Thelma and Louise*

## Sex and Different Cities

They did not know each other and they lived in different cities, but Anna, Sylvia and Francesca were living parallel lives. While they were young, each had been attractive and had been approached by men over and over again. Mike had fallen for Anna, and he was a catch, but she was not in love. John had *fallen for Sylvia and proposed to her on a trip to Tahiti, but she was not in love. Richard had fallen for Francesca and on the eve of their nuptials, she canceled, because she was not in love.*

*Each now lives alone, in her mid-forties with a career. Each is still waiting for Mr. Right.*

---

**GOLD-DIGGING GIRL FACT**

If you don't settle, you may end up with nothing.

*Dr. Daniela Drake*

---

Comparing the two stories, we can begin to decipher the previously undecipherable. In Lola's case, she "settled" because she didn't know what else to do. All her best girl-friends claimed they'd found their love bunny and said they were "deeply in love." (Many were, of course, lying.) On the other hand, Lola at 34 began to see herself as unmarriageable, and she soon began to worry that she would grow old alone and die with her cats. But Lola hadn't counted on the toll it would take on her psyche to be with someone she despised. And she hadn't realized after so many years of marriage how hard it would be to opt for someone else. In the second story, the women were only ten years younger than Lola and were more optimistic. They were the "have it all" girls. They may have loved their careers and were unwilling to "settle" for anyone but Mr. Right. So they settled on being alone, but only Sylvia had the foresight to freeze her eggs.

**GOLD-DIGGING GIRL QUIP**

Better alone than in bad company.

*Old Spanish Saying*

## Modern Marriage

Should we conclude that the whole concept of "settling" be rethought? If you're clear on what you want, say, a fun career that doesn't require 60-hour workweeks, a few children you can take off time to enjoy, some nice vacations, a somewhat posh lifestyle, then finding a man who can bankroll it and hold a decent conversation with you may just be hitting the modern-day jackpot. Forget Friday's "Fantasy Five" lottery ticket stuffed in your pocket—that may just be Mr. Right coming toward you right now with the craters in his face and the bulging wallet.

Don't forget that modern lasers can "correct" practically any "imperfection." Or you may just learn to love those acne pits, the receding hairline, or his dwarf-like stature. But this should not be thought of as "settling," or what they really mean by this: selling out by marrying "down." Instead, this can be seen as just one of the many new versions of having it all. And if someone dares to ask if you're in love (count on it, someone will ask) you could just point at him and say, "How could I be with him if I weren't?"

Girls, here's the point: get clarity on what you want, and by now that should not necessarily include falling in love. Look, by the time you read this book, you've probably been in and out of love a dozen times. You'll have written off some of this madness as "puppy love" or a "school girl crush"—but we both know the truth. It fades, doesn't it? Even in Rachel's case (Chapter 20), years after passion drove her to have sex with both Peter and his wife, she found she'd finally forgiven him for choosing someone else. She told us it was like shedding old lizard skin and finding out she was still new underneath.

---

Just as we are putting away the old-fashioned idea of "settling," there's something else to consider. In much of contemporary Europe the rates of marriage are way, way down. In 1950s America, married couples represented 80% of all households. By 2000 that number dropped to 51%, and in 2007 singleton households outnumbered married households for the first time in our history.[63]

What's causing this? Are women holding out for Mr. Right? If so, with our new notions of "settling for what you want" instead of vainly holding out for the one person to pin all your hopes and dreams on, then maybe the rates will rise again. Or, with so much "free milk" around, are men simply avoiding the hideous entanglements of marriage?

But in America, marriage is still revered, even if we enter into it through a revolving door. Recent surveys show that the majority of Americans of both sexes still believe that being married is the ideal.[64] And most demographers still think that 90% of Americans will eventually marry. That's good news for those girls who are beginning to understand that marriage has most often been about resources and wealth—and probably ought to be again. "Settling" is not *settling* for a man, but opting for a lifestyle and an agreeable companion. Academics might call her the "economic woman," but we like to think of her as a Gold-Digging Girl.

## BOTTOM LINE

A Smart Girl can't foresee the future, but she can clarify her goals and plan for her future.

## CHAPTER 26

# Forward Thinking

*The need for change bulldozed a road
down the center of my mind.*

MAYA ANGELOU, POET

Consider the male peacock fanning his iridescent plumes to attract the girls. "Don't hate me because I'm beautiful," the male lion seems to say as he shakes his alluring golden mane. And don't forget the stunning silver-backed male gorilla knuckle-walking back-and-forth to choose amongst the uniformly brown females.

"Males are bright and ostentatious because females are in demand and can afford to be choosy," biologist Richard Dawkins wrote in *The Selfish Gene*. He points out that humans are unique in the animal kingdom because the females—not the males—flaunt their looks to attract a mate. "What has happened to the modern western man?" Dawkins pondered. "Has the male really become the sought after sex, the one that is in demand? If so, why?" Even Dawkins, a genius famous for *knowing-it-all*, implies that this remains one of biology's great mysteries.

By now we know that women spend a fortune trying to look good and that men are transparently clear about their demands for a great looking mate. Even the most recent studies show that for men, attractiveness still ranks as the most important quality in a partner. On the other hand, for women, physical attractiveness ranks much lower when listing qualities in an ideal consort. While ancient biological imperatives and modern conventional wisdom predict that women want men with high earning power, in practice it isn't true.

Let's revisit the supposed bargain: women supply the babies, men supply the provisions. It makes sense. Men and women are built differently, have different biological aptitudes and contribute in their own way to the social order. It seems fair.

Dutifully, a modern gal might go bankrupt trying to look beautiful and sexy—in increasingly drastic ways. We'll put our lives at risk to plump our puckers, boost our breasts or revive our virginity. It appears the ladies are going *all out* to hold up their side of the deal.

And the guys? Well, at the risk of repeating ourselves again and again and again, somewhere along the way, the deal broke down. Women are now denounced as gold-diggers for desiring our balance of the bargain. These days most girls just hope to find a guy with a nice-fitting pair of pants and a job. So we've backed down, and conceded that earning power is important to us gals, but it doesn't trump emotional availability and personality.

Let's go back to Richard Dawkins' unanswered question, "How come humans have it all backwards?" Why do women work so hard to look good while plenty of guys lie around in sweat pants playing video games? In an effort to understand what Dawkins could not, we took a survey of young women who were working hard at looking good to see if they had some insight. Here are some of the answers:

1. Because women are smarter.
2. Because women are weaker and dependent on men.
3. Because we're independent of men.
4. Because we want the power to choose.

5. Because women are competitive.

6. Because there aren't a lot of good men around.

This was no longer what scientists call a "thought experiment." These were actual answers from pretty women out on the front lines in the battle of the sexes. Armed with lip gloss and eyeliner, these ladies didn't have time for deep thought. But remember the rule about test-taking: When puzzled, the first answer that pops to mind is usually right. So let's drill down on this survey and find out what insights these women offered.

First, men and women certainly have different competencies and interests, but are we smarter? We know for a fact that we aren't dumber. The guardians of IQ tests have been looking for proof of male intellectual superiority since the tests were first administered. If there were any statistical difference, do ya really think they would have kept that secret to themselves?

Second, are women weaker? And are we dependent on men? Looking at hunter-gatherer societies that live close to the land can clue us into the more animal dynamics between the sexes. In these societies, male hunters troop into town with fresh flesh dangling off shafts of wood—flashy emblems of their prowess with spears and long-sharp objects. There might be a party that night and maybe even a little lovin'. But truth be told, these big wins are random and cannot be counted on to feed the community. Instead, the female gatherers provide the majority of the food needs of the group. And the tools. And the clothing. And the childcare. So we can answer with conviction: women are not weaker nor are we necessarily dependent on men.

How did so many of us come to believe that we were? Perhaps because the back-breaking work of walking for miles and gathering seeds and nuts and fruit isn't very sexy, women swallowed the story that while females cowered in huts, we depended on men for food. But women have always been industrious. Not too long ago, when we were an agrarian society, women were considered so valuable that a man who wanted to marry had to pay a "bride price" to her family for the privilege. But things changed once the workplace became the province of men and women were relegated to domestic work that was viewed as unimportant. Next thing you know in order to tie the knot a woman had to come up with a "dowry" and pay the man to marry her!

Making payment to a man's family for marriage has and does still exist in many societies. Across the globe plenty of cultures have bought the line about women's inferiority hook, line and sinker. Yet, historically women have quietly been the backbone of most societies by bringing in much of the food and supplying many other needs of the group—shelter, earthenware, textiles, you name it. But these modest yet vital contributions count for little in the modern workplace that celebrates the male hunter culture and its big wins—the striped zebra carcasses dripping with blood. We've already shown that women, unless they act like men, don't thrive in this environment.

Now it's true that some hunter-gatherer societies have all-female hunter groups and others have women who join the male hunters.[65] Yet these arrangements are unusual. We suspect that these warrior women are the same dames who thrive in the male-dominated labor force. But for the rest of us, the workplace is not designed with our gathering tendencies in mind.

So we arrive at the third point: we can be independent. We are not the weaker sex, and we're not naturally dependent on men, we simply have different strengths. If need be we can make do on our own. So why aren't men fanning out their magnificent plumage to please us?

Dawkins' inability to solve this mystery may simply be that he asked the wrong question. This brings us to our fourth and fifth point: Women want the power to choose and we are competitive. With different skills and aptitudes, women and men are interdependent. In a dangerous world, having the mate that suits you best would provide a big survival advantage. Being beautiful grants a woman more choice in her mate. It gives her a survival advantage over her plainer female competitor. With our big brains, we're unlike beasts in heat that are willing to copulate with any male who shows up endowed with the largest antler. To partner up for survival, being sexy is to the woman's advantage in picking the very best mate for her.

### GOLD-DIGGING GIRL QUOTE

I live by a man's code, designed to fit in a man's world, yet at the same time I never forget that a woman's first job is to choose the right shade of lipstick.

*Carole Lombard, Actress*

While evolutionary biologists couldn't answer the seemingly puzzling question of the human reversal of sex roles, on a sunny afternoon a few young working gals in Los Angeles struck upon the answer that eluded male academics. Yes, we humans have it backwards, but for good reason. Our males and females are more equal than in other species. And both sexes need the power to select the right mate.

Oh, and one last thing: while half the guys are rockin' brews in dirty gym shorts with skid marks on their undies, and the other ones are hoarding wealth while throwing us out of the boardrooms, we gals do need to be competitive. We have nothing but anecdotes to back this up, but it does appear to be true: There aren't a lot of good men around. But the strange bonus for us ladies is that with these revolving door marriages, the "good guys" just keep going around and around and around.

———⚬⚬⚬———

Let's take one last step back and ask: How did the romantic dream get so out of hand? As Nicolas Cage's character said in the movie *Moonstruck*, "We are here to ruin ourselves and love the wrong people." Well, that was great advice for the movies, not real life. Yes, we *will* love the wrong people—simply because we can't help ourselves—but loving the wrong person doesn't have to wreck your life. Not anymore.

Falling in love does feel good, but the problems arise when we make it our number one priority. As women were relegated to less and less important roles in Western society, did it simply become our female focus—a malignant outgrowth of our primitive survival strategy for mate selection?

Is it the female version of the male greed cycle? The early humans who thrived probably had a compatible mate to help out with life's savage challenges. But their lives were short. Death ended most marriages before divorce does today.[66] But primitive instincts still drive us and we compete to find our "soul mates." We girls all want bragging rights to our own Cinderella story. All the young ladies in our survey said they loved Cinderella when they were little girls and hoped a Cinderella story would come true for them as women. The unmarried women were still hoping. The married women assured us that it was a fairytale indeed, right up there with Old St. Nick and the Easter Bunny.

So now that we're all up to speed, we ask again, "What's a smart girl to do?"

We say, use your Information Age brain and exploit your Stone Age instincts for survival. For now, it's a pretty safe bet that men are going to keep us out of the really high-paying jobs. If it's so important that they win and they won't level the playing field, then we'll work around it. We'll realign our values with theirs. If they're after money, status and power, then that's what we'll "love" them for.

Let's face it, this isn't an activist generation. Most people were against the shenanigans that went on after 9/11, but hardly a person took to the streets. We girls can't and won't protest or legislate our way out of inequality in the workplace. Nor will we prevent men from hitting the restart button at 40 to grab the jackpot of an energetic, young wife with gravity-defying boobs.

Since the entire country keeps blathering on about personal responsibility, then let's take individual action on behalf of our own individual lives—that's what will change the tide. We can bring about radical change, one gold-digger at a time. Won't it be nice to reward men for their industriousness? It's certainly more a mark of character than muscular arms or a winning smile.

By now, as good as being in love feels, smart girls know that romantic love isn't an emotion, it's a concoction of biology and instinct. Its effect fades. Smart girls know that even if they aren't spectacularly beautiful, all of us are evolution's winners, so we're all in the game. Smart girls know that we must take advantage of our fleeting youth, because both love and work are harder to find as we age. Smart girls know that we humans thrive on touch and companionship, but that's no reason to settle for a slacker who can't be bothered to call the next day.

So, ladies, let's do what we can with our brief time on earth and our even briefer youth. Build your friendships, treat yourselves kindly, get clear on your goals, and keep looking for Mr. Right, who just happens to be Mr. Rich.

## BOTTOM LINE

Smart Girls Marry Money.

# End Notes

[1] Peterson, Jonathan, "Old Story: Women May Have It Worse; Divorce and lost earning time could put living standards in a free fall late in life," *The Los Angeles Times*, December 28, 2006.; Rose, Stephen J., Hartmann, Heidi I. "Still a Man's Labor Market: The Long Term Earnings Gap." Institute for Women's Policy Research. January, 2004.

[2] Coontz, Stephanie. *Marriage, a History: How Love Conquered Marriage*. New York: Penguin Books, 2005.

[3] Mansfield, Harvey C. *Manliness*. Yale University Press, April 4, 2007.

[4] Falter-Barns, Suzanne. "Balancing Agendas: Work, Family and the Law." U.S. Society & Values, June, 1997.

[5] Neil, Dan. "The Devil's Playthings." *The Los Angeles Times*, November 18, 2007.

[6] See sources, interviews, anecdotes included in this work.

[7] Fisher, Helen. *Why We Love: The Nature and Chemistry of Romantic Love*. Holt Paperbacks, 2004.

[8] Ibid.

[9] Ibid.

[10] Mieszkowski, Katharine. *Happily Never After: Sex gets boring, eyes wander, but according to the author of "I Don't," knowing the history of marriage can help save yours*. Salon.com, August 9, 2008.

[11] Fisher, Helen. *Anatomy of Love: A Natural History of Mating, Marriage and Why We Stray*. Ballantine, 1994.; Buss, David M. *The Evolution of Desire: Strategies of Human Mating*. Basic Books, 2003.

[12] Woman's Day/AOL. Woman's Day/AOL Poll Reveals Majority of Married Women Would Reconsider Their Spouses. www.prnewswire.com, January 4, 2008.

[13] Buss, David M. *The Evolution of Desire-Revised Edition 4.* Basic Books, July 1, 2003. Reportedly, by the time they hit the age of 40, the Ache of Paraguay marry and divorce an average of 11 times.

[14] Buss. *Evolution of Desire.*

[15] Fisher. *Why We Love.*

[16] Buss. *Evolution of Desire.*

[17] Francese, Peter. "Working Women." *American Demographics.* March 1, 2003.

[18] Sullivan, Amy. "Why Didn't More Women Vote for Hillary?" *Time Magazine*, June 5, 2008.

[19] Rose, Stephen J., Hartmann, Heidi I. "Still a Man's Labor Market: The Long Term Earnings Gap." Institute for Women's Policy Research. January, 2004.

[20] Elsbach, Kimberly. "The Crying Game." *Sacramento Business Journal.* March 21, 2008.

[21] Unicef. The State of the World's Children 2007. Women and Children: The Double Dividend of Gender Equality. Inequality in Politics. http://www.unicef.org/sowc07/profiles/inequality_politics.php, accessed November 5, 2008.

[22] "Workplace Anger – Who Wins?" *Reuters*, August 3, 2007; Parsons, Claudia. "Angry Men Get Ahead, but Angry Women Get Penalized." *Reuters.* August 3, 2007.

[23] Ibid.

[24] Ibid.

[25] www.cbsnews.com. Accessed November 1, 2008. "Study: Work Incivility Rises: 25 Percent of Workers Have Chronic Anger." Aug. 12, 1999.

[26] Ibid.

[27] Bennetts, Leslie. *The Feminine Mistake: Are We Giving Up Too Much?* Voice Books. March 28, 2007.

[28] Maureen Dowd. *Are Men Necessary? When Sexes Collide.* Putnam Adult. November 8, 2005.

[29] Bureau of Labor Statistics; Crittenden. *The Price of Motherhood.*

[30] National Institute of Health. *Early Child Care Linked to Increases in Vocabulary, Some Problem Behaviors in Fifth and Sixth Grades.* March 28, 2007.

[31] www.courttv.com, accessed November 1, 2008. *Former day care owner gets five years for toddler's fatal overdose;* Updated October 28, 2005.

[32] Belkin, Lisa. "The Opt-Out Revolution." *The New York Times.* October 26, 2003.

[33] Cornell University News Service. Aloi, Daniel. *Mothers face disadvantages in getting hired, Cornell study says.* August 4, 2005.

[34] Crittenden. *The Price of Motherhood.*

[35] Crenshaw, Theresa L. *The Alchemy of Love and Lust—How Are Sex Hormones Influence Our Relationships.* Pocket, July 1, 1997.

[36] Etcoff, Nancy. *Survival of the Prettiest-The Science of Beauty.* Anchor, (Reprinted Edition), July 11, 2000.

[37] Buss. *Evolution of Desire.*

[38] Muller, Martin N. "Male Chimpanzees Prefer Mating with Older Females." *Current Biology.* Volume 16, Issue 22, 2234-2238, 21 November 2006.

[39] Maines, Rachel. *The Technology of Orgasm: "Hysteria," the Vibrator, and Women's Sexual Satisfaction.* Johns Hopkins University Press. March 1, 2001.

[40] Ibid.

[41] The female prostate, while largely ignored by practicing gynecologists, was officially recognized in 2002 by FICAT, the international board that names anatomical structures. However, the term did not appear in their publication until 2008. "The fact that FICAT intended to recognize a female prostate was a news story early in the century," wrote Colin Wedell-Smith, retired Professor of Anatomy at University of Tasmania in a personal communication. "But Terminologia Histolog-

ica has a 2008 publication date; its IBSN numbers are: ISBN 10: 0-7817-6610-9 and ISBN-12: 978-0-7817-66109-4." On page 65:

H3.06.03.0.00009 Glandula paraurethralis; Prostata feminina[92] Para-urethral gland; Female prostate

H3.06.03.0.00009 *Prostata feminine:* This term is introduced because of the morphological and immunological significance of the structure (Zaviacic M, Ablin RJ. The female prostate and prostate-specific antigen. Immunohistochemical localization, implications of this prostate marker in women and reasons for using the term prostate in the human female. Histol. Histolopathol 2000; 15:131-142).

"The anatomical terminologies that are published by FICAT are definitive and internationally recognized in their own right," Professor Ian Whitmore, Chairman of FICAT. (Personal communication.)

[42] Sundahl, Deborah. *Female Ejaculation and the G-Spot: Not Your Mother's Orgasm Book! (Positively Sexual.* Hunter House; March 24, 2003.)

[43] Ibid.

[44] Lloyd, Elizabeth A. "Research at Indiana University: Evolution of the female orgasm." www.research.indiana.edu, accessed November 8, 2008.

[45] Sundahl. *Female Ejaculation and the G-Spot.*

[46] Buss. *Evolution of Desire.*

[47] Small, Meredith F. "Are We Losers? Putting Mating Theory to the Test." *The New York Times.* March 30, 1999.

[48] Etcoff. *Survival of the Prettiest.*

[49] Liang, D. and Schal, C. "Volatile Sex Pheromone in the Female German Cockroach." *Cellular and Molecular Life Sciences,* April 1993; Leam, S. "Cockroach Tergal glands producing female sex attractant pheromone and male aphrodisiacs in particular subfamily Blaberinae (Blattaria: Blaberidae)". *European Journal of Entomology.* January 1, 2006.

[50] Sheehy, Gail. *Sex and the Seasoned Woman: Pursuing the Passionate Life.* Random House. January 10, 2006.

[51] Benedict, Carey. "A 'Senior Moment' or a Self-Fulfilling Prophecy?" *The New York Times.* July 18, 2006.

[52] Brizendine, Louann. *The Female Brain.* Broadway, August 7, 2007.

[53] Etcoff. *Survival of the Prettiest.*

[54] Ibid.

[55] Cassidy, John. "The Greed Cycle." *The New Yorker,* September 23, 2002.

[56] Ibid.

[57] Ibid.

[58] Ibid.

[59] Coontz. *History of Marriage.*

[60] Ibid.

[61] Ibid.

[62] Pinker, Steven. *How the Mind Works.* W.W.Norton & Company. January 1, 1999.

[63] Roberts, Sam. "51% of Women Are Now Living Without Spouse." *The New York Times.* January 16, 2007.

[64] Coontz. *History of Marriage.*

[65] Ibid.

[66] Ibid.

# Acknowledgments

We would first and foremost like to thank our agent Tricia Davey and editor Jennifer Kasius for believing in the idea and letting us run with it. We are also grateful to Stephanie Tade and Jeremy Katz who saw the book's merit and passed it forward until it found its home, and to Jason Kayser for his fabulous cover design and interior illustrations.

A huge thanks to our preliminary readers whose comments and suggestions were invaluable: Karen Brailsford, Julie Eagle, Diane DeMartino and Joanna Milter. We are also thankful to the many Smart Girls in our lives who shared their stories (you know who you are). Thanks also to Ben and Eric—without whom we would never have written this book.

We are also indebted and thankful for the insights, clarification and personal communication provided by those who contributed professionally to the work: Economics Professor Myra Strober, Economics Professor David Kreps, Ann Crittenden, Chairman of FICAT Professor Ian Whitmore and Anatomy Professor Emeritus Colin Wendell-Smith.

Special thanks to Daniela's much-beloved co-workers, Leticia Jimenez and Laura Arangure, who provided on-going support, encouragement and youthful inspiration. Thanks also for insight, perspective and laughter to Vanessa Arias, Myrna Viramontes, Gloria Villalobos, Maggie Sanchez, Juana

Esparza, Angelica Hernandez, Adriana Camarena, Ana Vargas, Gloria Barr, Ana Gerardo, Silvia Paz, Immer Escamilla, Jesus Carlos, MD and my language instructor Juan Morales. Special thanks to Hector Lastra for challenging and clarifying our thinking. Thanks to a couple of great doctors and certainly the greatest bosses in the world: Tim Gonzalez and Rob Blackman. A personal note of gratitude to my patients who I get to learn from and love every day. Thanks to all of you for turning work into a three letter word: joy.

Thanks also to those who took the time to lend their insights and time: Cyndee Ayson Mitchell, MD, and the girl-docs at Spectrum: Alain Park, MD, Allison Hill, MD and especially Yvonne Bohn, MD. Also, thanks to the ground-breaking work of Dr. Milan Zaviacic and Deborah Sundahl.

We so appreciate those who read the work and spread the word. Huge thanks and love to our sisters Diane Drake, Ginna Winkler, Mary Church and our moms Kris Seitz and Nola Drake. Big thanks to long-term writing partner, editor, advisor and dear friend Adam Fawer, and to Eric Lahey for his illustrations.

Musical inspiration was provided by Dave Matthews, Justin Timberlake and Kanye West. Thanks guys. Thanks also to: Cathy Griffen, Sarah Maizes, Christie Cole, Stephanie Gaynor, Carla Danella, Joanna Milter, Nusa Maal Coleman, Monica Maynerick, Nusa Maal, Dr. Rosina Samadani, Dr. Adrienne Burrows, Dr. Derrell Porter, Marco Nieuwenhuize, Edie Tolchin, Linda Friedman, Stephanie Hsieh, Elizabeth Gomart, Jill Franklyn, Randy Levy, Charlene Sarstedt, Albert Beveridge, Rob LaFranco, Patricia Coleman, Ana Leggeri, Cathy Opie, Julie Burleigh, Eden Rountree, Moira McMahon, Eduardo Maal, Tracy Verna, Stephanie Berk, Josie Viviano, Kirsten Kemp, Linda Barry-Esposito, Howard Samuels, Jorja Robin Davis, Eric Schulze, Kerri Randles, Melissa Mathison, Calista Flockhart, Carroll Gray, Mary Becker, Greg and Beth Winkler, and Norman Church. Love and special thanks to Elizabeth Baker Young, Sang Roberson, Annie Ferran and all the ladies at the "Queen of Hearts" national meeting in 2007. A shout out with gratitude to Hillary Harris for her love and photography. Thanks to Francesca Lia Block for her support, enthusiasm and her fabulous girl gang of writers.

Here's to the couples we know and admire: Jennifer and Rick Glassman, Rob and Karen Cowan, Rose Kuo and Larry Gross, John and Samantha Glenn, Elaine Holliman and Tom Kearney, Paul and Dana McCrane, Cathy Opie and Julie Burleigh, Matt Freeman and Greg Henderson, Liz and Sean Ruiz, Trish Blessing and Jeffrey Bell, Amber and Gavin Power. And special thanks to Carla Pennington, as a great mom and successful executive producer, you are an inspiration for future Smart Girls who will be married for their money!

We are grateful for the work of so many smart people who enlighten and inform: Maureen Dowd, Elizabeth Lloyd, Louann Brizendine, Nancy Etcoff, Stephanie Coontz, Susan Love, Jon Stewart, Malcolm Gladwell, Bill Maher, Milan Zaviacic, David Buss, Helen Fisher, Theresa Crenshaw, Ann Crittenden, Gigi Levangie Grazer, Carrie Fisher, Candace Bushnell, Lisa Belkin, Leslie Bennetts, Myra Strober, Naomi Wolf, Linda Hirshman, Richard Dawkins, Steven Pinker, Mike Spence, Mike Bishop, Harold Varmus and Stephen Colbert.

Thanks to our families who put up with hours, days, months of us knee deep in reading, researching and writing. Deep love and appreciation to David who was our rock and our cook. Thanks to our children, who have been waiting and waiting for this book to come out. They are our heroes, our light and our hope. Thank you Giulia, Miguel, and Ethan.

# Photo credits